Christianity and the Future of Welfare

Christianity

and the

Future of Welfare

DUNCAN B. FORRESTER

EPWORTH PRESS

7162 0409 6

First published 1985
by Epworth Press
Room 195, 1 Central Buildings
Westminster, London SW1

Typeset at The Spartan Press Ltd
Lymington, Hants
and printed in Great Britain by
Richard Clay (The Chaucer Press) Ltd
Bungay, Suffolk

In Grateful Memory of
My Parents
I.M.F. 1895 – 1976
W.R.F. 1892 – 1984

Contents

Preface

It is the shape of British society for at least a generation which is at stake in the contemporary debate about the future of welfare. No longer is it a matter of tinkering with the details of a system which is generally accepted as adequate in its broad outlines. The time for little adjustments here and there is past; today a radical reconsideration leading to far-reaching changes is inevitable. Already, in advance of any searching and widespread public debate, there have been alterations or even reversals of policy which have profound significance for the future. Two contradictory voices are heard: the one calls for an open debate about the kind of Britain we want to have, about who bears the cost and who reaps the benefits of social policies, about how to defend the interests of the vulnerable and the weak; the other declares that raising questions of social justice or fair distribution is a harmful distraction from the one thing needful – a thriving economy. If economic prosperity may only be achieved in the short term by encouraging the rich to get richer and the poor poorer, ultimately everyone will benefit. Both major protagonists in the present desultory debate seem wistful and nostalgic – in the one case looking back to the heady days of post-war reconstruction and the establishment of the welfare state in the 1940s, and in the other yearning for the economic and social policies of the 1920s, or even of Charles Dickens' England. The discussion so far has hardly measured up to the gravity of the crisis, the long-term significance of the issues, or the extent of the opportunities for imaginative leadership.

This book is primarily an invitation to Christians to join in the debate. Like their predecessors of a generation ago and more, they have a contribution to make and a clear responsibility to make it. The reason why this is so is very simple: the issues are closely related to the good news of the kingdom of God, and the outcome of the discussion will profoundly affect people and community life in Britain for years to come. So those who are enjoined to seek first the kingdom of God and his justice cannot afford to be detached from these matters.

A three-fold Christian responsibility is involved. First, there is the task of sustaining, renewing, clarifying, revising and commending a Christian social vision. This does not mean that there is such a thing as *a* (let alone *the*) Christian social theory; the Christian vision is at once more comprehensive and more poetic than any social theory. Nor is it the same as the 'Christian principles' that church leaders attempt to apply to social and political issues, although principles may indeed be derived from the Christian vision. Secondly, there is the tricky but unavoidable responsibility for relating the vision to current policy options, without dissolving the vision into a political manifesto or denying its contemporary political relevance. It is usually easier to discern that some lines of action are radically incompatible with the Christian vision, to say a prophetic 'No', than to affirm that a particular policy would be more or less unambiguously the implementation of a part of the vision. Hard work on the relation of the vision to policy is always necessary if Christianity is to avoid the twin dangers of a false politicization or a no less false privatization. Thirdly, the church has always had a concern for influencing people's attitudes and values, for encouraging the endeavour to 'bring every thought into captivity of Christ'. Inevitably this involves engaging with the attitudes and values which are expressed in political life, in voting, in decision making. In a democracy public opinion is of immense political significance; and the churches through their preaching and teaching and public pronouncements have a responsibility not to echo or amplify popular prejudices, but to endeavour to lead and shape public opinion.

This book is intended to open up some of the major issues which require discussion. These call for examination at a depth which is not possible within the compass of a short book, which is, in a way, a by-product of a more substantial reconsideration of equality as a Christian value on which I am engaged. There are, of course, other major issues of theory and of policy which require far more detailed and penetrating study than has been possible in this book. But I have written out of a sense of urgency and alarm at the raggedness of the debate thus far, the reluctance to engage with the profound conflicts of values and of world-views which underlie it, and the paucity of theological and Christian contribution. I have attempted to show that there is a Christian responsibility to engage with these matters, to discuss the manner of that engagement, and to outline what seems to me the agenda, with some provisional comments on the matters in dispute.

I am indebted to numerous friends and colleagues, particularly in the Edinburgh University Department of Christian Ethics and Practical Theology and the Centre for Theology and Public Issues, who have discussed the concerns of this book with me, and commented on synopses and drafts. I am particularly grateful to Dr Robin Gill who went through the typescript with meticulous care and suggested numerous improvements, and to Dr J. I. H. McDonald whose views on the use of the Bible in Christian social ethics I have found particularly stimulating and helpful. My wife, Margaret, and my children, Donald and Catriona, have been characteristically supportive to me in this project; without their interest and encouragement, and tolerance of my abstraction while the book was being written, it would never have seen the light of day. Tina Picton-Phillipps swiftly and accurately transformed my untidy drafts and scrawls into typescript. I am grateful to her.

University of Edinburgh   *Duncan B. Forrester*
October 1984

1

Christianity and
the Search for Welfare

When Sir William Beveridge's Report on *Social Security and Allied
Services*, the central part of the blueprint for the post-war welfare
state, was published in 1942 the Archbishop of Canterbury declared
that this was the first occasion on which an attempt was being made
to embody the whole spirit of the Christian ethic in an Act of
Parliament. He was no doubt rather carried away by the amazing
mood of popular enthusiasm which greeted the appearance of the
report. But a touch of exaggeration was pardonable in a statement
which so accurately reflected the widespread conviction that a
radically new social order must be established in post-war Britain,
and that this order should express values derived from the Christian
faith. The war was not only about the elimination of the obscenity of
Nazism; positively it was about the establishment of new societies in
which freedom, equality, fraternity and co-operation were to be the
dominant values and the whole community was to be engaged in
battle with the evils of poverty, disease, unemployment and so
forth, and committed to caring compassionately for those in need.
For many, many people Beveridge's Report and the other plans for
post-war reconstruction and the establishment of a welfare state
represented the ideals for which the war was being fought and the
hope which sustained the war effort. They were far more specific
and attractive than the airy generalities of the Atlantic Charter or
other statements of war aims. And when with peace there came the
time for implementation there was the excitement of embarking
upon a great social experiment. A whole generation echoed
Wordsworth:

Bliss was it in that dawn to be alive,
But to be young was very heaven!

British society was to be reshaped. Social problems would be tackled with the same determination and concentration of resources which had won the war. The fraternity and co-operation in the pursuit of a common goal which had won the war would also win the peace.

In the 1940s there was a strong national consensus spanning the major political parties and national institutions that a welfare state was desirable and necessary. Popular expectations were high, but sometimes conflicting. And this consensus served to conceal a good deal of vagueness and ambiguity. Some held a minimalist view of the welfare state, seeing it as hardly more than a new term for the pre-war forms of social provision and social order. Others held a maximalist view: the welfare state involved a revolutionary re-casting of British society and of the economy which would transform Britain into an egalitarian and socialist society. Since virtually everyone agreed that the welfare state was a good thing, it gradually became a kind of sacred cow, beyond all criticism, and it was easy to avoid hard questions about the meaning of welfare or the role of the state as against other agencies as a dispenser of welfare. The churches played a not insignificant role in the sustaining of this welfare consensus and, to be honest, shared also in the vagueness and uncertainty which the consensus served to conceal.

There is today in Britain and most of the other Western democracies a widespread disillusion with the welfare state as established in the 1940s and 50s. The great expectations of the previous generation have been replaced by disappointment. The welfare state is felt not to have lived up to its promises, not to have delivered the goods, to have failed to solve major social problems such as poverty, and indeed to have contributed to the exacerbation of the economic situation. Benefits, it is believed, have often gone to the wrong people, an unhealthy dependence has been engendered, and instead of a compassionate society of mutual care we have found a community riven with the 'money militancy' of rival powerful groups while those at the foot of the pile are all but forgotten. Some argue that the welfare state has been subverted; others that it has fallen victim to its inability to satisfy the inflated expectations which were invested in it, or to its own internal contradictions. We will examine this mood of disenchantment and

2

the attitudes and arguments which fuel it later on. For these things need to be taken seriously. Welfare is in crisis. The new ideological polarization means that the welfare state is attacked from right and left, with arguments which often betray a strange similarity, while there is only too little hard-headed and forward looking defence of welfare.

Our view is that the welfare state should be regarded as a notable and adventurous social experiment. Like all experiments it needs to be assessed, and assessed soberly and realistically, with a view to wise social planning for the future. It has produced many and great good things, but, like all such experiments, failures and mistakes as well. It has not brought the kingdom of God, nor has it succeeded in embodying the whole spirit of the Christian ethic in acts of Parliament. But it was a valiant attempt, an experiment, from which much may be learned. And Christians and the churches should involve themselves in this assessment, for they have a contribution to make, and a clear responsibility to make it. Christians should not be wistful, nostalgic people, longing for the heady days of the 1940s to come back again. Nor should they be timid about entering the debate about the future of welfare, incapacitated by secularization and the numerical decline of the churches. If Christianity has insights into human nature and destiny and the ability to inculcate motives and values into society, Christians have something distinctive to offer. They should assess the 'welfare experiment' as rigorously as possible, measuring it against Christian values and theological insights, and asking what may be learned, positively and negatively, from the experiment.

The perennial springs of a Christian concern with social welfare lie deep within the tradition. There are various strands which may be distinguished. Care for the victims and love for the neighbour here and now are seen as anticipations of the messianic expectation of the coming of the kingdom, of the acceptable year of the Lord, when God's will is manifestly done on earth as it is in heaven. Temporal and eternal welfare are not split apart, but closely related and human beings are always seen as persons-in-relationship rather than isolated individuals free from social ties. Thus justice and love are closely correlated in an order which seeks to reflect the divine love and justice so that loving one's neighbour is inseparable from doing justice. The different strands come together in the concept of *shalom*, a Hebrew term notoriously difficult to translate because it holds together in balance and complementarity so much that we in modern times tend to split apart. It denotes the human, and indeed

3

the cosmic, flourishing which characterizes the messianic age, outlined poetically in passages such as Isaiah 11 and 61, in which a new quality of fellowship is based upon reconciliation and righteousness. *Shalom* is a word which is as aptly, if not fully adequately, rendered 'welfare' as it is 'peace'. It is both a hope, and the present and partial realization of that hope. It relates both to social structures, to the way society is organized, and to personal relationships and individual responsibilities. Within *shalom*, love and fidelity have come together, justice and peace join hands and justice looks down from heaven (Ps. 85, NEB). In other words, welfare is inseparable from love, justice, fidelity and peace. The Old Testament assumes that the *shalom* of the individual cannot and should not be set against the *shalom* of the group; fellowship is an indispensable component of *shalom*, and it is in this fellowship that true freedom is to be found. *Shalom* is a gift of God, but not one that may be easily or glibly appropriated in this fallen world.

The New Testament has at its heart the affirmation that Jesus, who is, according to the writer of the letter to the Ephesians, our peace, our *eirene*, our *shalom*, has come into this broken and disfigured world. He suffered for our *shalom* – one translation of Isaiah 53.5 speaks of 'the discipline of our welfare being borne by Him'. And the risen Christ blesses his disciples with *shalom* – 'Peace be unto you' (John 21.21, 26) – establishing a fellowship, the church, in which the *shalom*, welfare, wholeness for which the whole creation groans in travail may be found amidst the brokenness of the present order as a sign, a promise and a partial manifestation of God's care for the welfare of all humankind. The New Testament therefore represents both a broadening and an anticipatory actualization of *shalom*, welfare. Certainly it is not confined in the New Testament to some artificial, individual, spiritual or institutional realm. Thus New Testament faith involves a commitment to seek the welfare of one's fellows and of human society.

Again and again down the centuries the understanding of *shalom* has been distorted or fragmented. False eschatology pushes it to a remote future without present referent or relevance. Naive idealism believes that *shalom* can be achieved without qualification or compromise in such a world as this, now. Often *shalom* has been spiritualized in such a way as to remove it entirely from the public, outward realm confining it in the personal, inward and subjective, or isolating it in cultic activity. A narrow individualism saw *shalom* as the generator of personal imperatives, but as having nothing to do with social structures or group relationships. Not only in the

4

Lutheran tradition, although most explicitly there, charity and justice were torn apart, and justice was declared the responsibility of the secular realm rather than a Christian or churchly concern. Even a nineteenth-century Calvinist of the eminence of Dr Thomas Chalmers could regard the social and political order as something God-given and beyond the purview of the church or prophetic theological scrutiny. For him – and this was indeed the majority view in post-Enlightenment Christianity – the church had a responsibility to dispense charity or relief to the 'deserving poor' within a scenario which was beyond question; the matter of justice was simply set aside. Even in the provision of charity the churches increasingly found themselves unable to shoulder the burden and handed responsibilities over to secular agencies. Thus the two strands of care for one's neighbour, compassion for the victims, a bias to the poor on the one hand, and the search for a more just and caring society on the other were torn apart, leaving the church in danger of imprisonment in a cultic ghetto of irrelevance.

Concern for *shalom* has taken various shapes throughout the ages, as Christians have endeavoured to respond to diverse situations and understand the gospel in the light of the issues of the day. Christianity does not produce ready-made and unchanging blueprints of a just social order. But it does provide a tradition of thought and concern, a perspective, an orientation and a motivation which, when brought together with the facts and serious analysis of the situation, are capable of generating proposals and policies. This book does not give detailed attention to the sources or development of a Christian concern with social welfare. Its purpose is more modest. First, we will examine the framing of the welfare state in Britain, giving particular attention to the Christian contribution and asking what lessons may be learned from this which are relevant today. Secondly, we will analyse the present mood of disenchantment with the welfare state, asking what went wrong (and what went right), and assessing the criticisms from Right and Left which are being offered. Thirdly, and finally, we will look at some of the major issues which arise for Christians out of the contemporary crisis of the welfare state and ask what kind of contribution Christians and theologians might, and ought to, make. Attempting to embody the spirit of the Christian ethic in acts of Parliament is an endeavour which can never be fully successful, but which Christians cannot abandon without a dangerous narrowing of their understanding of the gospel and a withdrawal of the faith from the public realm, which amounts to a kind of practical apostasy.

2

The Stirring of Conscience

Talk of the church as the conscience of the nation or the guardian of the nation's conscience is vague and seldom particularly convincing. Today in a plural society that has become largely secular it seems downright implausible to many people. Surely, the argument runs, the modern church must have a much more modest role to play. But, lest we dismiss the whole idea out of hand, two things should be said. First, it is necessary to remember that the Christian faith has down the centuries implanted and sustained values in Western cultures so that many or most Western values have at least an historical link with Christian faith, whether this is recognized or not. A strong case can be made out that Christianity continues to inculcate values, and that this is a vital function even in modern secular society.[1] And one may also argue that values require to be grounded in some sort of faith, and in a secular and pluralist society like Britain no viable alternative to Christianity is in sight. Religious faith implies values, and values have religious presuppositions. It is hard to see how the Christian church could *be* the church without attempting to see that society is shaped by Christian values. Secondly, one may argue that there is at present a vacancy in the role of 'guardian of the nation's conscience' which the church has a responsibility to try to fill. The moral passion which moved some political parties seems to be replaced today by doctrinaire partisanship; the trade unions have squandered their moral credit by indulging in too much money militancy and ruthless pursuit of their members' interests often forgetting the unemployed and the poorest sections of the community. If the church does not fill the gap, no other major institution seems inclined to do so. Professor David Donnison sees pressure groups and lobbies such as Child Poverty Action Group or Shelter (to which one might add Amnesty

International, Anti-Apartheid and countless others) together with community action groups as playing a vital role here. 'They are', he writes, 'a forum in which the evolving moral standards of a civilized society and its governments are formulated and asserted. They have taken over the moral leadership of Britain from our emptying churches and our increasingly pragmatic political parties.'[2] Without dissenting from Donnison's assessment of the importance of such groups we would suggest that they are too small and too fragmented to act as 'guardian of the nation's conscience' on their own; they must relate to major institutions such as the churches if they are to be effective – and, furthermore, a church which denies an interest in their concerns has abandoned a large part of its social responsibility.

The church is embedded – sometimes comfortably, sometimes restlessly, as a leaven, an irritant, or a balm – in society. It is, accordingly, seldom easy to distinguish 'the Christian conscience' from 'the conscience of the nation'; the two have been wound together for so long that a process of assimilation, almost osmosis, has gone on for centuries. Our concern here is not to unravel this tangle, but simply to point out that conscience, even Christian conscience, tends to slumber and reconcile itself to the most nightmarish situations. It is stung into alertness by events and experiences which awake it from its complacent slumbers. And most really notable theology has been like that – elicited by some crisis which shattered conventional assumptions, brought new truths into view, and cried out for interpretation. Thus Augustine, contemplating the fall of Rome and the controversy that ensued, wrote his great *De Civitate Dei*; Reinhold Niebuhr's Gifford Lectures, *The Nature and Destiny of Man*, were delivered as the Second World War broke out and the crisis of Western civilization demanded interpretation; Karl Barth's massive theological project must be understood in part as his response to the horrors of Nazism.

Three happenings this century seem to have been of particular significance in arousing a deep and conscientious unease among Christians, and many others as well, about the absence of welfare, about the extent of poverty, ignorance, squalor and deprivation in society. Each of them brought people who were not themselves poor, but often privileged and influential, into personal human contact with those who were suffering from poverty and other social ills, with the victims, with those at the foot of the pile. This elicited a capacity to empathize, which led to anger, thought, and action. People discovered that in the midst of conditions of great injustice and degradation seeds of a different and a more caring society could

7

be found, seeds which must be nurtured and allowed to flower, seeds which gave the hope on which planning could be based. These experiences sparked off a powerful and resilient determination, widely diffused throughout the community but particularly strong among the working class, among intellectuals, and among Christians, that human degradation must be ended and welfare provided for all.

1. Rending the veil of ignorance

> The sufferings of the poor are, indeed, less observed than their misdeeds; not from any want of compassion but because they are less known; and this is the true reason why we so often hear them mentioned with abhorrence, and so seldom with pity. . . . They starve, and freeze, and rot among themselves, but they beg, and steal and rob among their betters. (Henry Fielding)[3]

Ignorance about the scale and effects of poverty was endemic among the British middle and upper classes in the nineteenth and early twentieth centuries. Much poverty was invisible. The prosperous rarely visited the slums; managers often showed no interest in the conditions in which their workers lived. Geographical, social, occupational and educational separation created a veil of ignorance. When it was pierced, when true reports of conditions on the other side penetrated into the middle class world, a common reaction was fear, combined with efforts to blame the poor for their own condition. Poor Law provision always drew a sharp division between the minority of the 'deserving poor', and the vast majority who 'had brought poverty and disaster upon themselves by their fecklessness, drunkenness, and immorality'. The treatment meted out to the two categories did not differ all that much; even the deserving poor were to be strongly discouraged from abandoning efforts at self-help, and relaxing in the 'comfort' of the work-house! Conditions were to be stringent, if not outright punitive, for both categories, lest 'the surplus population' (Scrooge's phrase) become too great a drain on the national prosperity, or a threat to the established order of things.

There were, indeed, pioneering efforts to portray the true state of the poor and of the urban proletariat. Henry Mayhew's researches on 'London Labour and the London Poor' provided startling documentation of the state of things in the metropolis in the middle of the nineteenth century, which was published in the *Morning Chronicle*. Engel's *Condition of the Working Class in England* (1844) was soberly factual, and concentrated on the mill towns of the north. Charles Booth's monumental *Labour and Life of the People, London*, first published in two volumes in 1889 and 1891, and later vastly expanded, attempted sytematically and statistically to chart the extent of poverty in London. General William Booth's *In Darkest England and the Way Out* (1890) produced a sensational account of the condition of the 'submerged tenth' which assumed that the root cause of the condition of the poor was sin, meaning the personal sin of the victims. The main emphasis, however, was on solutions: the Salvation Army needed resources if it were to offer redemption to the huge 'population sodden with drink, steeped in vice, eaten up by every social and physical malady'. But none of these really impressed on the middle class mind or on the political establishment the gravity and scale of the problem or the inadequacy of the responses on offer or proposed. There were moments of near panic, it is true, when revolutionary hordes were expected to emerge from the slums to ravage England, or when it was discovered that three-fifths of those offering for military service in the Boer War were unfit – a sad reminder that it is often only in war time that a nation recognizes that its greatest resource is people, and that people need care. Corners of the veil of ignorance were lifted momentarily but the reality that was glimpsed behind was so disturbing that people on the whole did not want to know and could not conceive of an adequate policy response.

Actual experience of conditions in the inner city slums was another matter, which for a whole range of significant intellectual, political and church leaders drew back the veil of ignorance, pricked their consciences, and led to their putting the provision of welfare and the tackling of the great social problems of the cities high on their personal agendas. Academic idealists who saw their task as the forming of an elite of 'Guardians' to lead and reshape British society (and the Empire, of course) sent a succession of students to the East End to find out what poverty meant and what could be done about it by living and working in settlements such as Toynbee Hall. Most of the dons were slightly heterodox Hegelians and rather liberal Christians: prominent among them were T. H. Green, Edward Caird and A. D. Lindsay, but there were many others and they were to be found in most universities. The settlements had their limitations, of course. The old woman whose home was in a slum near Toynbee Hall who exploded, 'If there's one thing I hate it's being lived among', had picked up a patronizing note. But whatever the effects of settlements on the communities in which they were established may have been, they had a profound impact on the thought and the life commitment of many who lived and worked there for a spell. William Temple, William Beveridge, R. H. Tawney, Clement Attlee and countless others were shocked and transformed by their disturbing encounter with the social reality of the cities, with human brokenness and the callousness of society and government to what was happening. Clergy in slum parishes had similar experiences, and their reports disturbed the church.

The rending of the veil of ignorance revealed a situation which was clearly not one that could be remedied, or even coped with, by private charity along with Poor Law provision; measures more radical by far were needed to respond adequately to such vast human need, and to mould one community out of the two nations which existed in such ignorance and fear of one another. But even in the crying scandal of the slums the students often found a quality of fellowship which gave a hint of what might characterize the society of the future. Meanwhile they put their energies into bodies like the Workers' Educational Association, the Fabian Society, and the Christian Socialist movement.

2. *The long weekend between the wars*

The soldiers who fought in the First World War were promised that they would return to a land 'fit for heroes to live in'. In many ways the war was not seen as a 'people's war', and the horrors of trench warfare in particular, with its prodigious cost in human lives taught some soldiers an abiding distrust of their aristocratic senior officers. In the aftermath of the war disillusion spread rapidly as the Depression began to bite, and many 'heroes' found themselves without jobs and in poverty while around them were the signs of the luxury and affluence of the wealthy minority. For a major part of the population the inter-war years were a time of disappointed hopes, often of real hardship, and the frustration, mounting on occasion to despair or apathy which follows upon long term unemployment. To the working class the Depression suggested a callousness about the welfare of men and women almost as great as had the bloody trench battles of the war.

Welfare provision was, and was intended to be, minimal, and means-tested relief for temporary distress and hardship. It was purely palliative, making no pretensions to solve social problems or remedy social ills. It was experienced as humiliating and sometimes even as punitive, and it did nothing either to solve the problem of poverty or to reduce the stigma of being poor. Indeed its scale and the way it was offered were intended to be strong incentives to seek employment and to escape from poverty, using the Victorian methods of self-help and self-improvement. But for the vast majority this emergency exit was locked and double bolted. Massive cuts in social provision in the 1920s and 30s were greeted (how familiar this sounds today!) with enthusiasm by much of the popular press which complained and campaigned against 'waste' in the social services, denounced scroungers, and called for even harder treatment of the poor, together with more swingeing cuts. 'Much irreparable damage has been done', pontificated the *Daily Telegraph* when welcoming a reduction in out-relief, 'in breaking down the old attitudes of independence. So long as out-relief is made easy there will be ever lengthening queues of persons lining up to receive it and grumbling at the inconvenience of having to wait their turn'.[4] The poor and the unemployed were blamed for their own predicament. The solution lies largely in their own efforts, it was asserted.

Then, as now, poverty and unemployment were remote from the direct personal experience of the majority of people in Britain. Those in work did not do at all badly, and the already prosperous tended to prosper exceedingly. The gap between the rich and the poor widened, but the realities of poverty and the consequences of unemployment were hidden from the prosperous and the powerful except when events such as the 'Jarrow Crusade' brought the condition of the unemployed briefly to the headlines. Poverty and unemployment, then as now, were not evenly spread geographically: the distressed areas were the North, Wales, Scotland, Lancashire and so on; the South-East, the area around the centre of power, was markedly more prosperous. The unemployed bore the brunt of the cost of the Depression, and bore it at a time when many prospered. Britain was clearly two nations, with ignorance, suspicion and distrust between them.

Not surprisingly, more and more questions were asked about a system which operates in this way, about the costs of the Depression, and how these costs were allocated, about a society which tolerates luxury in the midst of human degradation. Consciences were pricked in the 1930s. The sufferings of the unemployed seemed to demonstrate beyond the possibility of question that the market and free competition on their own could not provide a just, or even a tolerable, social order.

3. Warfare and welfare

The deep and vivid interest of the people of Britain in the kind of Britain which is to emerge when the floods of war subside . . .

11

implies no unwillingness to make all the sacrifices required for victory. It represents simply a refusal to take victory in war as an end in itself; it must be read as a determination to understand and to approve the end beyond victory for which sacrifices are being required and the purposes for which victory will be used. (Beveridge)[5]

Britain entered the Second World War in a chastened mood. The First World War had started as a crusade and ended in disillusion and deprivation for many. This time it was as if there were an implicit condition in the nation's willingness to fight against Hitler: that promises of a better future should not be made, only to be broken as soon as peace was restored. The hardships of the Depression had left a deep scar on the consciousness of the British working class; there must be no post-war return to the conditions of the 1930s.

The war was a time of hardship and suffering of a very different sort from the Depression. In it many people found seeds of hope and intimations of a better social order. For one thing, the sufferings and the sacrifices were shared more or less equally throughout the society. No one group bore a disproportionate share of the costs, as had the unemployed in the 1930s, and few were able to profit at the expense of their fellows. In all sorts of ways, some of them quite superficial, but others with profound implications, social barriers broke down. A new sense of national community and interdependence was experienced, and this fellowship and mutual care in the light of a common purpose was found to be good:

> There was less reserve among neighbours, and everyone seemed to be in and out of one another's houses, papering over pinpricks of light in blackened windows, claiming access to stairways and roofs, keeping meaningless records of alerts and all-clears, drinking cups of tea at all hours and, increasingly as time went on, arguing about the sort of Britain they wanted after the war.[6]

People were thrown together in a quite new way. Most of the middle classes had been insulated from the sufferings of the Depression, except when a hunger march passed through their suburb, or they read about the conditions of the unemployed in the papers. Through the programme of evacuation in the early period of the war, many middle class people had their first face-to-face encounter with what poverty and slum conditions did to children. 'Here were two nations confronted. The rich were chastened by this sudden revelation of social misery, and the young wanted to put an end to it.'[7] As an immediate consequence, there was general approval for school meals and for the provision of milk and orange juice and cod liver oil for all children.

People of different classes fought side by side, shared the same shelters, ate the same rations. The common goal, the sharing of sacrifices and the sharing of joys in its pursuit, produced a new quality of fellowship. Churchill promised only blood, toil, tears and sweat; but in return the people hoped for a new kind of society in Britain, in which the welfare of the whole community would continue to be the dominant concern of politics. It was as if a tacit contract had been reached between government and people: in exchange for sacrifices for the war effort, government would ensure that the dark days of the Depression would never return, and would devote some of its energies even in the darkest days of the war to planning for the new post-war Britain.

Revulsion against Nazism's contempt for other races and its radical inegalitarianism made fertile soil in which ideals of human equality could take root. But the lessons of the war went far beyond an ideological nausea at Hitlerism, a determination that the dark days of the Depression should never return, and a longing to perpetuate the new-found equality and fellowship in struggling for a common cause. It was not just that sacrifices now must earn their reward in the shape of a juster social order. A vision of a new system emerged, a vision which proved attractive precisely because it had already been experienced in part. For the 'warfare state' was a welfare state, and its welfare functions could surely be continued and extended in time of peace. Vested interests had been subordinated to the common good. Government had found a new role in mobilizing the resources, human and material, of the nation for war, helping men and women, long unemployed, to a recovery of dignity through sharing in the national effort, controlling the economy, and ensuring the fair distribution of scarce resources. The state was seen as capable of acting on behalf of the whole community, not for some sectional interests, and, as a consequence, the whole understanding of the scope of government was enlarged along with a conviction of the beneficence of state action:

It was increasingly regarded as a proper function or even obligation of government to ward off distress and strain not only among the poor but among all classes of society. And because the area of responsibility had so perceptibly widened, it was no longer thought sufficient to provide through various branches of

13

social assistance a standard of service hitherto considered appropriate for those in receipt of poor assistance.[8]

George Orwell summed up widely held views when he argued that 'the inefficiency of private capitalism has been proved all over Europe. Its injustice has been proved in the East End of London'.[9] Beyond that, 'what this war has demonstrated is that private capitalism . . . does not work. It cannot deliver the goods'.[10] It must be replaced by a planned economy and a welfare state, a new socialist society which 'will retain a vague reverence for the Christian moral code, and from time to time will refer to England as "a Christian country"'.[11] Even those who did not share Orwell's specifically socialist commitment for the most part hoped for comprehensive provision as of right for citizens in need, and a more just, equal and caring social order. The mood of expectation was captured immediately after Dunkirk by a notable leader in *The Times*:

> If we speak of democracy, we do not mean a democracy which maintains the right to vote, but forgets the right to work and the right to live. If we speak of freedom, we do not mean a rugged individualism which excludes social organization and economic planning. If we speak of equality, we do not mean a political equality nullified by social and economic privilege. If we speak of economic reconstruction, we think less of maximum production (although this too will be required) than of equitable distribution. . . . The new order cannot be based on the preservation of privilege, whether the privilege be that of a country, of a class, or of an individual.[12]

The war period established two particular emphases which were for long to be taken for granted as self-evident truths, but are now once more open to question. First, the conviction that the state is an effective guardian of the common good and should be the principal provider of welfare. The war had immeasurably increased people's expectations of what the state could deliver and confidence in its integrity and altruism. The old cautious and negative understandings of the state – whether as a 'dyke against sin' or as a 'night-watchman' – were for the time forgotten: the state that had won the war could win the peace; the waging of warfare had shown how the state alone could ensure welfare. This confidence in the state helps to explain why there was so little revolutionary feeling. In the second place, the experience of the war stimulated a new thirst for

equality as an architectonic value in British society. Universalism in
the provision of social services was one expression of this impulse.

These three traumatic experiences proved in their different ways to
be the birth-pangs of the modern welfare state by arousing the
conscience of the nation and by stimulating a determination that
there should be no going back to the past. They were also
experiences which issued in a call for a new *moral* structure of
society and provided vital hints and clues as to the nature of that
new social order. Uncontrolled capitalism had been shown in the
Depression incapable of providing even a minimum standard of
welfare for the people. It had divided and enervated the nation and
its means tested doles and grudging welfare provision had been
experienced as degrading. The war had demonstrated that a better
way was possible, that a society restructured on a new and moral
basis could work. Christians were not slow to affirm that the vision
glimpsed during the war and the call for post-war reconstruction
were Christian things, and to help in first shaping, and then
implementing, the vision.

3

The Building
of the Welfare State

Politicians liked to speak of the 'mosaic' of the Welfare State; in reality it was more of a crazy paving. What was done – and it was a lot – was the result of truly noble vision, but inevitably circumscribed by the country's economic situation, by the continuing barriers and preoccupations of class, by the nature of traditional welfare institutions, and by the perceptions planners had at the time of major social issues, perceptions clouded by a knowledge of life as it had been, rather than by an understanding of life as it would be. (A. Marwick)[1]

1. A question of terms

Richard Titmuss, who is very properly regarded as the leading theorist of social welfare in post-war Britain, strongly disliked that 'indefinable abstraction' the Welfare State. He used the term in the title of one of his books only after much pressure from his publisher, and he insisted that it should be put in inverted commas. He believed that the term put too much emphasis on the state's role in the provision of welfare, that it allowed people to think of welfare as a burden upon society, imposed from above, that it suggested that some final, satisfactory and coherent pattern of welfare had been developed in Britain.[2] He is right that the term may be systematically misleading or so emotionally charged as to be rather dangerous as a tool for description or analysis. But it is probably indispensable as a kind of short-hand term for 'that synthesis of past pragmatism and future aspirations which was the achievement of social policy in 1948'.[3] It was, in other words, the undeniably inadequate label for the vision which took shape in the war years and found its partial

16

fulfilment under the Labour Government of 1945.

The term 'welfare state' was coined by Professor Alfred Zimmern in the 1930s and used by William Temple as a central concept in his later political writings. Temple assumes that the 'night-watchman' state is a thing of the past; it is inevitable and desirable that the state should play a fuller role than had been allocated to it by classical liberalism, and its ability to do so had been abundantly demonstrated. Temple suggests that there is a choice between a 'welfare state' and a 'power state'. He is not so naive as to believe that you have a welfare state which does not exercise power, nor does he have manichaean notions that power as such is evil; he regards the new totalitarianisms as regimes which regard the pursuit of power as the overarching and sufficient end of political activity. Temple enquires as to the purposes for which power should be used and concludes that welfare should be high among the goals of politics. A welfare state, then, should be regarded as a society in which the government accepts positive responsibilities for social welfare and sees its function as doing battle with the five 'giants' that Sir William Beveridge saw as threatening British society – want, disease, ignorance, squalor and idleness. Asa Briggs gave a classic minimal definition:

> A 'welfare state' is a state in which organized power is deliberately used (through politics and administration) in an effort to modify the play of market forces in at least three directions – first, by guaranteeing individuals and families a minimum income irrespective of the market values of their work or their property; second, by narrowing the extent of 'social contingencies' (for example, sickness, old age and unemployment) which lead otherwise to individual and family crises; and third, by ensuring that all citizens, without distinction of status or class are offered the best standards available in relation to a certain agreed range of social service.[4]

The state, that is, intervenes on behalf of the community to ensure that the welfare of its citizens is not entirely at the mercy of the economic system's workings. But it is more than a social security state providing services for certain groups with specifiable needs; its concern is for the whole society and its welfare facilities are for the most part available to everyone. It does more than help people to provide for the needs of their families and themselves, or establish a 'floor' below which no member of the society can be allowed to fall: it is intended to be a kind of egalitarian social engineering, encouraging some degree of redistribution of resources within the society, greater equality of opportunity, and a measure of positive discrimination to help the victims of multiple deprivation and work towards a more equal situation. The welfare state is not intended to take over all responsibility for welfare from voluntary agencies, the family and the individual, but rather to ensure through the use of state power and state resources that in areas such as health, education, housing and transport, services of high quality are available to everyone and are dispensed in relation to need rather than income. In addition the state also accepts responsibility for encouraging a high level of employment and making available resources for those suffering from disability or involuntary hardships.

The welfare state is the result of a long and often difficult evolution away from the minimalist understanding of the state, in which there was little recognized role for political regulation or oversight of the economy, and such concern for welfare as there was was divided between private charity and punitive and degrading statutory provision for the poorest. The slow development of statutory welfare provision and the fascinating tale of the growth of the ideology which eventually came to undergird the welfare state are complex matters which cannot concern us here. All we must do is note that the idea of the welfare state as it emerged in Britain, and almost simultaneously in most of the industrialized democracies, includes a commitment to democracy; participation and freedom as well as equality and compassion are underlying values. And citizenship was subtly redefined: in a welfare state citizenship involves responsibility for the welfare of all one's fellow citizens, and the right to expect the community to respond to one's need. The state might take the initiative and have a continuing responsibility to monitor what was going on, but the intention was to create a more fraternal, just, equal and caring society. 'The idea of the welfare state', wrote David Thomson, 'is the apotheosis of a couple of centuries of political activity guided by the ideal of human equality and social justice.'[5]

2. William Beveridge

Sir William Beveridge with his succession of wartime reports caught the popular imagination and crystallized the vision in a remarkable way. Here was a David who took on simultaneously the five Goliaths that threatened British society, armed only with some pebbles of economic and sociological data and a meticulous concern for detail. Beneath lurked values, patrician rather than populist, but appealing to vast numbers of people. He was able to capitalize on vast and immediate public support for his proposals. A few regarded them as utopian or even dangerous. Churchill wrote in a cabinet note:

> A dangerous optimism is growing about the conditions it will be possible to establish here after the war. . . . Ministers should in my view be careful not to raise false hopes as was done last time by speeches about 'Homes for Heroes' etc. . . . It is because I do not wish to deceive the people by false hopes and airy visions of Utopia and Eldorado that I have refrained so far from making promises about the future.[6]

But for most people in the early 1940s to resist or question Beveridge's plans was rather like the Israelites in the wilderness questioning the authority of Moses as he strode down Mount Sinai with the tables of the law in his arms.

Beveridge was quite clear from the beginning that he was concerned to produce a *comprehensive* set of proposals. His first report, published despite a great deal of government and civil service reluctance, in 1942, was on social security, but Beveridge argued that its effectiveness would depend on the establishment of a National Health Service, the maintenance of full employment, and the inauguration of family allowances. He asserted that his plans involved nothing less than a revolutionary change in British society:

> The first principle is that any proposals for the future, while they should use to the full the experience gained in the past, should not be restricted by consideration of sectional interests established in the obtaining of that experience. Now, when the war is abolishing landmarks of every kind, is the opportunity for using experience in a clear field. A revolutionary moment in the world's history is a time for revolutions, not for patching.
>
> The second principle is that organization of social insurance should be treated as one part only of a comprehensive policy of social progress. Social insurance fully developed may provide income security; it is an attack upon Want. But Want is only one of five giants on the road of reconstruction and in some ways the easiest to attack. The others are Disease, Ignorance, Squalor and Idleness.
>
> The third principle is that social security must be achieved by co-operation between the State and the individual. The State

19

should offer security for service and contribution. The State in organizing security should not stifle incentive, opportunity, responsibility; in establishing a national minimum, it should leave room and encouragement for voluntary action by each individual to provide more than the minimum for himself and his family.[7]

According to Beveridge's specific proposals, the stigma of the hated means test was to be removed as quickly as possible so that benefits might be obtained by those in hardship *as a right*. The need for a means tested National Assistance provision was to be gradually eliminated by progressive rises in the level of national insurance benefits. A minimum income floor, below which no citizen should be allowed to fall, was to be established. The minimum income level was fixed rather low by Beveridge, but when the substance of his proposals was made law, the level was lower still. As a consequence a considerable and increasing number of people continued to rely on means-tested benefits – National Assistance, Supplementary Benefit, or the later Family Income Supplement. Beveridge and the resultant legislation firmly entrenched the new principle of universality: all employed people contributed to National Insurance, and Beveridge seemed to assume that this would involve an element of redistribution from the more prosperous to the poor. It has turned out otherwise.[8] In addition to social security provisions the Beveridge proposals insisted upon firm action to ensure full employment – an objective also high on the agenda of the new Keynesian orthodoxy. A National Health Service offering a high quality of care to all, a major campaign to improve housing conditions, and a reform of the educational system completed the blue-print of Beveridge's welfare state.

Beveridge spoke of his proposals as revolutionary, and it became commonplace to speak of 'the Beveridge revolution'.[9] But was it really a revolution? Beveridge himself was no revolutionary. He was a liberal, not a socialist, although by a series of historical accidents his ideas became substantially identified with the policies of the Labour Party. He did not profess to be a Christian, and was never a member of a church, although his values he identified as essentially Christian. He was committed to what he called 'practical religion', which was shaped by his devotion to 'the personality and spirit of Christ', but involved a scepticism about dogma and had no place for a church.[10] He accepted, with only minor qualifications, the 'Five Christian Standards' which four church leaders had proposed in the letter columns of *The Times* as criteria by which economic and social policies might be judged. This involved him endorsing an attack on *extreme* inequality in wealth and possessions, and supporting equality of educational opportunity, the safeguarding of the family, a restoration of a sense of vocation to work, and stewardship in the use of the earth's resources.[11] He was certainly no egalitarian, and did not put social equality high in his list of priorities. Nor did he suggest a thorough-going policy of economic redistribution. His proposals hardly amounted to a blueprint for revolution, but they did suggest a series of significant moves in the direction of a more equal, caring and fraternal society. He stood in the noble succession of imaginative social reformers, fundamentally committed to gradualism. It is significant that his proposals, while they aroused unprecedented enthusiasm in large sections of the population and encountered persistent opposition from government and civil service did not appear to *frighten* anyone, probably because they were not seen as a threat to existing structures of economic and political power.

The Beveridge proposals were criticized at the time for being too extensive, too expensive, and too radical; and later on, for not going far enough, for failure to effect significant redistribution, and for perpetuating 'obsolete free-market values'. But Beveridge's 'Grand Design' was never applied. Beveridge had intended the standard rates of benefit, unlike previous schemes, to be fixed just above subsistence level so that it would be possible to live on them without other resources. In fact ever since the 1948 Act the standard rate has been below the officially accepted poverty line, so that the scheme has never had the radical impact on poverty that was desired, and has had to be complemented by other systems of relief on a basis to which Beveridge was fundamentally opposed. Other crucial aspects of Beveridge's proposals were implemented grudgingly and in part, or not at all. The 'Grand Design' resolved itself into a relaying of the crazy paving, with some attractive flagstones added or replaced.

3. The welfare consensus

The 'vision splendid' of the welfare state was, we would argue, rooted in Christian values. But its specific shape and the possibilities of its implementation depended upon a particular set of historical circumstances. We have given some attention in Chapter 2 to three of the influences which led to the emergence of the vision. Its implementation was only possible because of other factors which encouraged this kind of social experiment – in particular the new forms of economic management associated with the name of Keynes, a period of sustained economic growth, and the existence of a strong national consensus in favour of the welfare state.

The Labour Party was swept into power in 1945 not simply by a convincing majority, but by what amounted almost to a national consensus. Churchill was nearly alone in seeing the war period as a temporary reversal of the proper ordering of society, which would be restored as before as soon as the war was over. His alarmist statements that his erstwhile cabinet colleagues of the Labour Party were secret totalitarians who would bring in the Gestapo in refurbished form, and Hayek's more academic argument that the way towards a greater equality and more public provision of welfare was 'the road to serfdom',[12] convinced few; they merely delayed the time when most Conservatives would declare themselves committed to equality and the welfare state as understood by Beveridge. The consensus expressed a new conviction that it is the responsibility of the state to provide for the welfare of all its citizens and ensure the maximum possible fairness and equality in the distribution of the nation's resources. Both those looking for a radical change in British society and paternalistic, one-nation Conservatives could support it. The Labour Party did not create the consensus; it inherited it. But it hoisted Labour to power and sustained the party until 1950, by which time it had become apparent that all the main political parties now accepted the consensus and were committed to the maintenance of the welfare state and the encouragement of equality, variously understood.

In the early post-war years the consensus represented something of a continuation of wartime solidarity. It was hoped that much of the old sense of common purpose could be maintained, that 'Dunkirk spirit' could be applied to the issues of post-war reconstruction, that the new Britain would continue the sense of fellowship which so many had found a liberating experience in the war years. No party which stressed class warfare or conflicts of interest could hope to represent the popular consensual mood. The Labour Party, following Beveridge, stressed *universality* of welfare provision rather than 'soaking the rich', or any other divisive or contentious policies, and thus kept in tune with the popular mood. Like all consensual politics, this was rooted in the middle ground and had an inbuilt tendency towards caution which made it, in broad outline, acceptable to politicians of varying hue long after the first flush of energetic reform by the Labour Government had been exhausted. The need to maintain the support of the consensus circumscribed radical governments: measures which might prove divisive or contentious were not infrequently quietly shelved, and it was recognized that progress must needs be slow because of the necessity to take 'the country' with the government. And at a time when scholars like Daniel Bell and Lipset were writing – prematurely, as it turned out – the obituary of ideology, serious discussions of principles or even examination of the ideological and practical tensions and incompatibilities within the welfare/equality consensus became unfashionable. Woolly thinking was allowed to go unchecked, and policy makers looked in vain to the intellectuals to suggest a critical theoretical undergirding for policy. People who sought for a theory or philosophy of equality and the welfare state rarely found anything to satisfy them. The welfare state began to appear to some as a cumbrous and haphazard amalgam of diverse and sometimes incompatible forms of social provision which did not have enough coherence to merit the label that was applied to it. And equality was used in such diverse senses that it served to confuse rather than illumine.

The Labour Party, having carried through a major programme of reform in the late 1940s, seemed to run out of steam and oscillated between euphoria and uncertainty. Many socialists did not know where to go next after the implementation of the programme of the 1945–50 Government. It was widely felt that an irreversible and highly desirable social revolution had been carried through, that Britain had become a markedly more equal society, most of Beveridge's giants had been slain or at least severely disabled, and all that was left was a tidying-up operation and the conservation of the gains already made. Even Tawney, in the Epilogue he added to *Equality* for its fourth edition in 1952, felt that the time was ripe for feelings of modest pride, for since the war the country had moved substantially in an egalitarian direction. There had been significant achievements as the result of following in general outline his 'strategy of equality'. Some redistribution of wealth along with the development of the 'collective provision' of the social services and public control of the economy had ensured that 'a somewhat more equalitarian social order is in process of emerging'.[13] Major social problems had been faced and tackled, and there was room, if not for complacency, then for some gentle self-congratulation. Vested interests had shown that they could not stop the people getting what

23

they wanted, and Tawney was confident that the people would not relinquish their welfare state or resile from the search for a more equal Britain.

The late 1940s to the early 70s was a period of extraordinary ideological consensus in British politics. All the major parties accepted the desirability of the welfare state. The Labour Party might implement the more important measures of social reform, but in general these (unlike nationalization, which had been an integral part of Tawney's 'strategy for equality') were accepted by the Conservatives, and sometimes a Conservative government did a good deal to streamline the operations of the social services. Political rhetoric suggested that there was a fundamental difference in the way the two major parties saw the welfare state, Labour viewing it as an instrument of social engineering helping to bring into being a more equal Britain, while the Tories saw it as primarily a floor, or safety net, for the most deprived. But if one looked at actions rather than rhetoric the differences between the parties became so blurred as to be almost indistinguishable. Both parties had a commitment to equality as a social goal. It would be tempting to suggest that Labour saw equality in social and economic terms, while the Conservatives emphasized equality of opportunity. But the contrast is by no means as sharp as that might indicate; many Labour politicians were primarily interested in equality of opportunity and showed real hesitation about promoting egalitarian policies which might be divisive and rock the boat. It has been forcefully argued that the Labour Party became less and less interested in measures of redistribution as the years went by and moved away from a serious commitment to egalitarian measures.[14] It was widely assumed that governments of whatever party would pursue over a wide range of issues virtually the same policies:

Over the longer run they would all try to increase industrial investment and improve Britain's lagging productivity, to secure some broad agreement about the distribution of incomes, to get unemployed people back into jobs, to free poorer people from means tests by giving them adequate benefits as of right, to give children a better start in life and more equal opportunities for the future, and to provide better care and support for the most vulnerable people and for families living on low or modest incomes. 'Middle England', we assumed would not tolerate any radical departure from these aims. A government which allowed – let alone encouraged – a return to high unemployment, the

24

social conflicts and means tests of the late 1930s could not survive.[15]

'There is a cracking sound in the political atmosphere', wrote Richard Crossman in December 1970, 'the sound of the consensus breaking up'.[16] He had an ear for the future, for within a decade the cold winds of economic adversity had broken the consensus apart. Within a few years both equality and the welfare state, from being things to which almost everyone paid at least lip-service, became highly controversial and had to look hard for friends to defend them. For twenty years the major parties had represented slight differences of emphasis and there had been little fundamental questioning of the value of equality or the desirability of the welfare state. The churches, with their instinctive dislike of conflict, had rejoiced in the consensus about domestic policy and turned most of their political attention outward, to engage with issues of decolonization and the cold war. Now all that was changed. The coming of harder times forced the realization that economic growth and prosperity had allowed the nation to salve rather than heal problems, and to conceal even from itself that it had abandoned the serious pursuit of a more just and equal society for the relentless search for higher living standards. The Labour Movement's concern for the poor and the weak seemed more a matter of political rhetoric rather than action and even the rhetoric was denied by the 'money militants' of the trade unions with their determination to maintain or enhance differentials.

The vision was fading.

4

Christian Contributions

The complex story of Christian contributions to the making of the modern British welfare state and the development of Christian attitudes to welfare remains to be told. This chapter makes no claim to do more than sketch three different contributions, each of which is significant in its own right and may have lessons, positive and negative, to teach us which are relevant to the development of a Christian response to the contemporary crisis of welfare. The various roles of the church in the public arena – as sustainer of visions, custodian of the nation's conscience, implanter of values, chaplain to the powerful, legitimator of policies, prophetic critic – were less problematic in the 1930s and 40s than they are today, for reasons we will discuss in Chapter 6. To repeat the prophecies or the solutions of a previous generation is little more than wistful incantation and shows scant regard for the particularities of a changed situation. But we can learn from a past generation's endeavours to respond to the needs of the day, and discern the signs of the times in the light of the gospel, lessons which may sharpen our response and deepen our understanding of how the Christian faith may be brought to bear on social and political affairs. We will focus on three functions which were peculiarly important contributions to the emergence and implementation of the idea of a welfare state: first, the affirmation and defence of fundamental Christian social values, with particular reference to the work of R. H. Tawney; secondly, the shaping of policies intended to express these values, focusing on the role of William Temple; and, thirdly, the mobilization of church support for welfare policies and the churches' backing for the 'welfare consensus', using Principal John Baillie's 'Commission for the Interpretation of God's Will in the Present Crisis' as the example.

Christian Contributions

1. Richard Tawney and Christian values

The essence of all morality is this: to believe that every human being is of infinite importance, and therefore that no considerations of expediency can justify the oppression of one by another. But to believe this it is necessary to believe in God. (R. H. Tawney)[1]

Richard Tawney was a mildly eccentric donnish figure who taught economic history for most of his working life at the London School of Economics. When he was presented for an honorary degree at the University of Oxford he was compared to Diogenes, the Greek philosopher who lived ascetically in a barrel, because Tawney and his wife had spent much of the war period living in a wooden hut that had once been a henhouse. He refused the peerage offered him by Ramsay MacDonald: 'No cat ties a tin can to its own tail', he said. His students loved him and he exercised tremendous influence through them, through his wide circle of friends, and through his involvement in the Workers' Educational Association and the Labour Movement. It is tempting to call him a saint, although the saintly idiom of politics is hardly current in Britain; but certainly he was the political and moral *guru* to several generations of radicals.

His scholarly writings were not particularly voluminous, but were (and are) influential. His *Religion and the Rise of Capitalism* (1926) examined and applied to the British scene the thesis associated with the names of Max Weber and Ernst Troeltsch, that Protestantism, particularly in its Calvinist form, was the nursing mother of capitalism. Tawney's efforts were also devoted to developing the theme that with the rise of capitalism and the possessive individualism on which it rests, theology and the church evacuated the economic sphere, abandoning any effort to shape and control economic activity on a Christian and moral basis. This was a theme he had already touched upon in rather general terms in the final chapter of *The Acquisitive Society* (1921). There he argued that the church and theology had withdrawn into the private and domestic realms from all serious and thoughtful engagement with public issues. The vacuum thus created was occupied by another 'creed', 'a persuasive, self-confident and militant gospel proclaiming the absolute value of economic success'.[2] This new gospel Tawney saw as destructive of fellowship and, in the strict sense, a false gospel, a modern paganism radically opposed to Christianity. 'Compromise is as impossible', he wrote, 'between the Church of Christ and the idolatry of wealth, which is the practical religion of capitalist societies, as it was between the Church and the State idolatry of the Roman Empire.'[3] But a watered down Christianity found it only too easy to compromise with the values of capitalism; it is not surprising that Tawney often despaired of the institution of the church. But throughout his life his writings contained clarion calls to Christians to recover the fullness of the gospel and realize that Christianity is not only concerned with the destiny of the individual soul but with the establishment of fraternity, justice and compassion in society.

Tawney is universally recognized as a moralist as well as an historian and social theorist. What is not always understood is how consciously and explicitly his values are grounded in Christian faith. His *Commonplace Book* reveals this more clearly than his other writings. 'The social order', he wrote there, 'is judged and condemned by a power transcending it.'[4] Social criticism, in other words, really presupposes some kind of religious belief. And he is absolutely clear and emphatic that morality requires belief in God. From the Christian faith he believed he had derived his concept of the good society – a fraternal fellowship of free equals, caring for one another:

> In order to believe in human equality it is necessary to believe in God. It is only when one contemplates the infinitely great that human differences appear so infinitely small as to be negligeable (sic). To put it [an] other way, the striking thing about man is that he is only a *little* lower than the angels themselves. When one realises this it is absurd to emphasise the fact that one man is, even so, lower than another. . . . What is wrong with the modern world is that having ceased to believe in the greatness of God, and therefore the infinite smallness (or greatness – the same thing!) of *man*, it has to invent distinctions between *men*. It does not say 'I have said, "Ye are gods"'! Nor does it say 'all flesh is grass'. It can neither rise to the heights nor descend to the depths. . . . What it does say is that *some* men are gods, and that some flesh is grass, and that the former should live off the latter (combined with pâté de foie gras and champagne), and this is false.[5]

This kind of theological argument is not to be found in some of Tawney's most influential writings, notably *Equality* (1931). But this is a profoundly Christian book although there is hardly any *explicitly* Christian language or theological reference in it. He is appealing to what Orwell called 'the deep tinge of Christian feeling' which characterizes the British people (or so Orwell believed) even if they have little explicit religious belief or practice. Writing in an increasingly secular society, Tawney feels the need to tailor his argument to make it accessible to secular readers. The underlying vision and the basis for the values is acknowledged to be Christian, but Tawney believes he can commend it in secular terms. Like many other classics of social and political thought, Tawney's *Equality* was published as a passionate manifesto or tract for the times in the midst of a major crisis; it was the Depression which so wonderfully concentrated his thinking and made him search for the values that would undergird a better form of society. He knew that the debate about social values was one from which Christians could not responsibly abstract themselves. His own contribution lay mainly in commending Christian values in secular terms and attacking the pagan values of mammon worship which he believed dominated capitalist society. But he also laid responsibilities for promoting social criticism and hopes for a better, juster, and more equal order of things squarely on the shoulders of the churches. The issue is fundamentally a religious one, and 'the proper bodies to propagate it are the Christian Churches'.[6]

The equality which Tawney espouses is equality of consideration, the idea that every human being has an equal claim to respect. All human beings by virtue of their common humanity have an equal right to provision for their needs, and society should seek to cultivate this common humanity by putting stress on institutions and procedures which 'meet common needs, and are a source of common enlightenment and common enjoyment'.[7] Equality does not mean a dreary sameness, nor does equality of treatment mean identity of treatment; indeed Tawney's vision of equality is one which encourages that lusty flowering of individuality which is only possible if inequalities are substantially diminished.

Equality, for Tawney, is the necessary basis for fraternity. Inequality divides communities and creates all sorts of barriers of suspicion and rivalry. Extreme inequalities

> divide what might have been a community into contending classes, of which one is engaged in a struggle to share in advantages which it does not yet enjoy and to limit the exercise of economic authority, while the other is occupied in a nervous effort to defend its position against encroachments.[8]

Thus inequality is destructive of fellowship by breaking the ties of fraternity and common purpose and by setting groups and individuals in conflict and competition with one another. Equality of opportunity, the *carrière ouverte aux talents*, a meritocratic society, is no solution. It does not in any way substantially alter the structure of society, but stimply makes the 'plums' slightly more generally accessible. And even that is more apparent than real, for Tawney is perfectly aware that only in a more equal society can some people's handicap at the starting post be provided for. Equality of opportunity is a kind of social lightning conductor which deflects some of the anger and damage engendered by inequality, but does no more. It obscures some of the more glaring and obnoxious symptoms of the 'disease of inequality' at the expense of making the infection even worse. Equality of opportunity is ridiculed as the 'Tadpole Philosophy':

> It is possible that intelligent tadpoles reconcile themselves to the inconvenience of their position, by reflecting that, though most of them will live and die as tadpoles and nothing more, the most fortunate of the species will one day shed their tails, distend their mouths and stomachs, hop nimbly onto dry land, and croak addresses to their former friends on the virtues by means of which tadpoles of character and capacity can rise to be frogs. This conception of society may be described, perhaps, as the Tadpole Philosophy, since the consolation it offers for social evils consists in the statement that exceptional individuals can succeed in evading them.[9]

For Tawney equality is not antithetical to liberty but essential for its diffusion and maintenance. Frequently, he believes, liberty has been regarded in far too narrow a fashion and without social controls to ensure that one person's freedom is not used to harm others or restrict their freedom. 'Freedom,' he said in another of his aquatic metaphors, 'for the pike is death for the minnows.'[10] Liberty must be extended rather than being regarded as the possession of one class or group. Freedom and equality are complementary to one another. Tawney clearly has no time for an equality imposed in such a way as to diminish or destroy freedom; indeed that would not for him be equality at all. And liberty he sees as 'equality in action' – all are equally protected against the abuse of power, whether that power be political or economic. Liberty and equality must be held in balance, Tawney believed, as the twin piers on which the edifice of a fraternal society would be reared. If he says less about freedom than he does about equality it is because he sees it as being less in need of defence and because he believes that the neglect of equality has led to a narrow and distorted understanding of freedom. Policies which Hayek later denounced as 'the road to serfdom' Tawney saw as the way to enlarge the scope of freedom for the vast majority of the populace at the cost of restricting the freedom of the strong to do what they want at the expense of the weak. Freedom, he held, involved equality of status but it also required diversity of function.

Tawney was not a Utopian who believed that the immediate realization of total equality at whatever cost was either desirable or possible. His plea is that society should take equality as one of its objectives and make moves in the direction of greater equality even if absolute equality was quite out of the question. The present degree of economic and social inequality he regarded as unacceptable, because it was socially divisive and individually dehumanizing. Social goals matter and are important even if they are never fully attained:

> What matters to the health of society is the objective towards which its face is set, and to suggest that it is immaterial in which direction it moves, because, whatever the direction, the goal must always elude it, is not scientific but irrational. It is like using the impossibility of absolute cleanliness as a pretext for rolling in a manure heap, or denying the importance of honesty because no one can be wholly honest.[11]

Accordingly the task is to diminish inequality with all deliberate speed in order to permit human individuality, freedom and fellowship to flower. And to this end he proposes a 'strategy of equality'.

Here Tawney moves from the realm of values to the realm of politics. He was aware, as many of his disciples in the 1940s were not, that any serious moves towards equality would encounter determined resistance from vested interests which, if they could not stop egalitarian policies, would attempt to subvert them. He also believed that capitalism was inherently inegalitarian, so that egalitarian policies were subversive of capitalism and should be recognized as such. In welfare measures which were no more than palliative he had little interest; in addition to the extension of the social services there must be measures of substantial redistribution of economic and political resources, and the economic system must be made more responsible and accountable to the public. Furthermore it would be necessary to reform radically the educational system and in particular to abolish the private schools, so quaintly called 'public schools' in England: the system is

at once an educational monstrosity and a grave national mis-
fortune. It is educationally vicious, since to mix with companions
from homes of different types is an important part of the
education of the young. It is socially disastrous, for it does more
than any other single cause, except capitalism itself, to perpetuate the division of the nation into classes of which one is almost
unintelligible to the other.[12]

The strategy involved controlling the commanding heights of the
economy in the public interest, extending the system of social
security and using it explicitly, in a way Beveridge hardly recognized, as an instrument of social engineering, reforming the
educational system to ensure that it did not continue to perpetuate
privilege and inequality, and ensuring through taxation that differences of wealth and income were progressively reduced.

Here was a plan for a welfare society founded on Christian and
socialist principles and going far further than Beveridge's liberal
understanding of the kind of social changes that should be
introduced in Britain. Tawney's manifesto, partly because of the
magnificence of the style and the cogency of the argument, but
particularly on account of the compelling power of Tawney's
passion for justice, had a deep and continuing impact. He deployed
few, if any, overtly Christian arguments, perhaps because he was
addressing himself to a society which was increasingly secular. But
his own commitments were known and he played a major role in the
development of the churches' social thinking in the 30s and 40s.[13]
And those who cared to probe below the surface of a book such as
Equality found a motivation and a set of values which were
profoundly Christian. The influence of his thinking was immense,
upon students of sociology and social policy such as Richard
Titmuss and Peter Townsend who continued his investigations in
poverty and inequality, upon politicians, primarily but not exclusively of the Left, and upon churchmen and theologians such as his
life-long friend, William Temple.

Tawney's ability to hold together a 'utopian' vision of a fraternal
society free from exploitation and injustice, with a hard-headed
realism about political and economic realities and made him
concerned with the strategy and tactics of realizing that vision in
partial fashion, is of lasting significance. His conviction that the
Christian vision generates social values which stand in sharp
opposition to the operative values of possessive individualism, but
are often tamed and domesticated in capitalist societies, has been

challenged but not fundamentally shaken by the New Right. His challenge to the churches to think hard and rigorously about the social implications of the gospel and to struggle to communicate Christian values and the Christian vision in a plural and secular society speaks also to this generation.

2. William Temple and the shaping of policy

William Temple 'was able to relate the ultimate insights of religion about the human situation to the immediate necessities of political justice and the proximate possibilities of a just social order more vitally and creatively than any other modern Christian leader.' (Reinhold Niebuhr)[14]

Reinhold Niebuhr, writing just a few days after Temple's death, may have been guilty of a little exaggeration, but he points to the fact that Temple was himself a seminal social theologian and provided leadership and stimulus to a remarkable renaissance of Christian social thinking in Britain, and more widely as well.

Temple, like Tawney and Beveridge, was a Balliol man, and the three were personal friends. The link between Temple and Tawney was particularly close. They had been school fellows and in politics they were well to the left of Beveridge. Both played a major role in the Workers' Educational Association, and both were members of the Labour Party until Temple, to Tawney's disgust, withdrew on being appointed Bishop of Manchester, believing that a bishop should not be identified with partisan politics. Temple was, however, throughout his life a convinced socialist, and it has been said with justice that *Christianity and Social Order* contains the most sustained defence of socialism and the most detailed socialist programme ever written by a British churchman of his rank.[15]

Temple's status as far and away the outstanding British church leader of his generation was both his strength and his weakness. That he was successively Bishop of Manchester, Archbishop of York, and then, for a brief but crucial period during the war, Archbishop of Canterbury ensured that his voice was heard and that he had access to the corridors of power. There is no doubt that he had enormous influence on the framing and passing of the Education Act of 1944, and on a whole range of social policies, mainly concerning post-war reconstruction. It is probable that his position led him to trim or temper his views on some issues to a certain degree, but what is remarkable is the extent to which he managed to combine the roles of prophet and church leader. In

Christianity and Social Order he makes a clear formal distinction between what is proper and necessary for the church, and its accredited leaders, to say on political and social issues, and the more problematic, controversial and partisan views which the individual Christian may adopt. With a certain panache he relegates to an appendix the policies he would, as an individual Christian like to promote, saying that while the substance of the book should be generally acceptable to Christians 'it is most improbable that every Christian should endorse what I now go on to say'.[16] But when we compare the substance of the appendix with the final chapter of the book, 'The Task Before Us', it is the close similarity which impresses; the appendix adds little more than details, and it is hard to see it as in any way more controversial than the rest of the book.

Temple's major theological writings were in philosophical, not social, theology. Until he somewhat modified his views as a result of ecumenical involvements and an awareness of the relevance of Barthian theology on the continent, he was a theologian of an idealist sort, to whom the more philosophical idealism of T. H. Green, Caird, and the 'Balliol men' was highly congenial. The interests of Balliol idealism in social issues of course meant that Temple's theology was never totally detached from such matters, but most of his major contributions in this area come in the latter part of his life.

As an idealist philosopher of religion he argued that the incarnation provided, as it were, the projection which would enable a unified map of reality to be constructed. His thought tended to be optimistic, progressivist and rather moralistic. All this was shaken by the rise of Nazism and the outbreak of the Second World War seeming to confirm the attack on liberalism associated with the names of Karl Barth and Reinhold Niebuhr. Temple in 1939 declared that it was impossible to make a map of such a broken world as this; the Christian task was to convert the world. Temple's theology now became almost Barthian, more concerned with the pervasiveness and the gravity of sin and the need for redemption, less sanguine about an historical evolution to the kingdom. How far his new theological views were transposed into his social thinking remains doubtful, but they certainly seem to have induced a new awareness of the dangers of power and the limits of political action.

As a church leader and social thinker increasingly involved with the developing ecumenical movement, Temple was encouraged by colleagues such as Reinhold Niebuhr and J. H. Oldham to work on social theology in close co-operation with social scientists. Tawney, as we have seen, was a life-long friend and major influence. John Maynard Keynes commented in detail on the draft of *Christianity and Social Order*. His response is so interesting, and so encouraging to Temple's efforts to create an economics based on Christian principles, that it deserves full quotation:

I should have thought that in Chapter 1 you understated your case. Along one line of origin at least, economics more properly called political economy is on the side of ethics. Marshall always used to insist that it was through ethics that he arrived at political economy and I would claim myself in this, as in other respects, to be a pupil of his. I should have thought that nearly all English economists in the tradition, apart from Ricardo, reached economics that way. There are practically no issues of policy as distinct from technique which do not involve ethical considerations. If this is emphasised, the right of the Church to interfere in what is essentially a branch of ethics becomes even more obvious.

I should have thought again that you were understating your case in the third chapter, where you consider the past record of the Church in these matters. I should have supposed that it was a very recent heresy indeed to cut these matters out of its province. Are you not going too far in suggesting that in the XVIII Century the Church accepted this limitation? I should have thought decidedly not. Leaving out the Scots, such as Hume and Adam Smith, and foreign residents in London, such as Mandeville and Cantillon, I can think of no one important in the development of politico-economic ideas, apart from Bentham, who was not a clergyman and in most cases a high dignatory of the Church. For example, Dean Swift interested himself in these matters. Bishop Fleetwood wrote the first scientific treatise on price and the theory of index numbers. Bishop Berkeley wrote some of the shrewdest essays in these subjects available in his time. Bishop Butler, although primarily of ethical importance, is not to be neglected in this field. Archdeacon Paley is of fundamental importance. The Reverend T. R. Malthus was the greatest economist writing in the XVIII Century after Adam Smith. I agree that unless one includes Laud there are not many Archbishops before yourself to be included in the list. But Archbishop Sumner's early work was on economics.[17]

Besides Keynes there were numerous other social scientists of eminence and ability who felt sufficiently at one with what Temple was trying to do that they were happy to work with him. He never did his social theology in isolation. From 1924 when he acted as the presiding genius over the Conference on Christian Politics, Economics and Citizenship ('COPEC') in Birmingham, he was at the heart of a remarkable circle of experts and practitioners. The most notable fruit of the style of co-operative working for which Temple was the catalyst was the report on long-term unemployment, *Men Without Work*, published in 1938. Soundly based on empirical studies, the report had impact in Whitehall and gave Temple empirical backing for the case for Family Allowances. His circle of social scientists tried, on the whole successfully, to ensure that Temple, as an amateur in the field, did not make obvious gaffes. Their co-operation with Temple makes one hesitate to accept the accusation of Sumption and Joseph that Temple refused to consider the practical consequences of the measures he advocated[18] or Suggate's suggestion that he had a 'persistent tendency to drift into moral deductions from the principles without the requisite attention to the facts of the case'.[19] Temple was almost neurotic about the right of the church to 'interfere' in social, economic and political matters, and very aware of the dangers of a superficial moralism or an unrealistic pietism. He had undoubtedly been much criticized for some of his interventions; but friends like Tawney and Keynes gave him courage by their assistance and by their welcoming of what he was trying to do.

Christianity and Social Order starts with a defence of the church's right to 'interfere' and a general indication that the existing order should be challenged as incompatible with 'Christian principles'. Prominent among these criteria is equality. In rather unguarded language Temple writes, echoing Tawney:

. . . apart from faith in God there is really nothing to be said for the notion of human equality. Men do not seem to be equal in any respect, if we judge by available evidence. But if all are children of one Father, then all are equal heirs of a status in comparison with which the apparent differences of quality and capacity are unimportant; in the deepest and most important of all – their relationship to God – all are equal. Why should some of God's children have full opportunity to develop their capacities in freely-chosen occupations, while others are confined to a stunted form of existence, enslaved to types of labour which represent no personal choice but the sole opportunity offered? The Christian cannot ignore a challenge in the name of justice.[20]

Temple next proceeds to present a series of Christian principles: first, basic principles which are really theological propositions about God and the nature and destiny of man; and then, secondary principles derived from the fundamental principles, these being in fact, values and moral principles of a very general sort. Temple lists them as freedom, fellowship and service. After some discussion of the problems involved in the implementation of principles in politics, Temple distils out of the more general Christian principles a set of guidelines or objectives for government, which he believes to be founded upon the Christian gospel and hopes will be implemented in post-war Britain. Together these outline an egalitarian welfare state, and are worth quoting in full:

1. Every child should find itself a member of a family housed with decency and dignity, so that it may grow up as a member of that basic community in a happy fellowship unspoilt by underfeeding or overcrowding, by dirty and drab surroundings or by mechanical monotony of environment.

2. Every child should have the opportunity of an education till years of maturity, so planned as to allow for his peculiar aptitudes and make possible their full development. This education should throughout be inspired by faith in God and find its focus in worship.

3. Every citizen should be secure in possession of such income as will enable him to maintain a home and bring up children in such conditions as are described in paragraph 1 above.

4. Every citizen should have a voice in the conduct of the business or industry which is carried on by means of his labour, and the satisfaction of knowing that his labour is directed to the well-being of the community.

5. Every citizen should have sufficient daily leisure, with two days rest in seven, and, if an employee, an annual holiday with pay, to enable him to enjoy a full personal life with such interests and activities as his tasks and talents may direct.

6. Every citizen should have assured liberty in the forms of freedom of worship, of speech, of assembly, and of association for special purposes.

. . . Utopian? Only in the sense that we cannot have it all tomorrow. But we can set ourselves steadily to advance towards the six-fold objective. It can all be summed up in a phrase: *the aim of a Christian social order is the fullest possible development of individual personality in the widest and deepest possible fellowship.*[21]

Christianity and Social Order is not a great book of theology or of social thinking. But its influence in shaping the conception of an egalitarian welfare state was considerable, and it did much to mobilize public opinion in the pursuit of such an objective. It has fairly been called 'one of the foundation piers of the Welfare State' by the economist Denys Munby.[22] It demonstrated the strengths, and the weaknesses as well, of the 'middle axiom' approach in the doing of social theology. And one can trace its (and Temple's) quite specific influence on certain aspects of post-war reconstruction, particularly, but not exclusively, in the Education Act of 1944.

3. The Baillie Commission

Everybody knows now that, whether we like it or not, the life of our country, and the life of all the Western nations, is going to wear after the war a complexion very different from that of the life so familiar to us in pre-war days. . . . Weary of a day when every man was his own master, men are seeking out new forms of community. . . . 'How,' we ask, 'can men be drawn to a Gospel whose one practical expression is serving Christ by serving the least of His needy brethren, if we preach it in abstraction from the crying needs of the poor and oppressed of our own society?' (J. Baillie)[23]

In 1940 the General Assembly of the Church of Scotland established a 'Commission for the Interpretation of God's Will in the Present Crisis' which was popularly known as the Baillie Commission after its convener, the Edinburgh theologian and church leader, Professor John Baillie. The Commission had a grandiloquent title and a wide-ranging remit, but it managed to focus its work in such a way that its annual reports between 1941 and 1945 attracted considerable attention and comment outside as well as within the churches. The Commission numbered among its members many of the most prominent Scottish theologians and church leaders, but although there was a fair proportion of Elders few of them were notable for their expertise in social science or their eminence in public life. Baillie's leadership left its mark on the work of the Commission. He had been a colleague of Reinhold Niebuhr in Union Seminary, New York, and the two men were very close to one another theologically. Baillie was deeply involved in the work of the ecumenical movement and he encouraged the Commission to use in its consideration of social and political issues the 'middle axiom' method which had been developed in a series of ecumenical conferences in the 1930s. In its general approach the Commission was, therefore, close to Temple, but there were also significant differences of emphasis, some of which arose from the Calvinist theology which underlay the Scottish Commission's work. The Baillie Commission, for instance, felt no need to apologize for 'interfering' in social and political matters; it worked within a tradition which affirmed very strongly the universal sovereignty of Christ and rejected the Lutheran theory of the two kingdoms and the Anglican tendency to see the church as in some sense the servant of the state rather than its prophetic critic. The whole of life was to be subject to the gospel, and Calvinism was seen as having a peculiar contribution to make to post-war reconstruction: the Calvinist tradition's 'explicit renunciation of the ecclesiocratic or Hildebrandine ideal, its frank concession of a real autonomy to the various secular interests, its acceptance and indeed eager championship of the principle of religious freedom and, more generally, its complete conversion from the conception of a compulsive to that of an open Christian civilization, have, in spite of the new problems and perils which they have brought in their wake, turned out on the whole to be sources of increased solidarity and stability'.[24]

In dealing with equality, the Commission's report was quite explicit. Ideals such as this have tended to be parted from their Christian roots and take on an independent existence. Sometimes the church has even forgotten that equality is an implication of the gospel; now equality must be *repossessed* as a Christian value: 'We are all equal because we are all made in God's image, because we are all sinners, and because for us all Christ died. It is not that I am as good as my neighbour, but that I am as sinful as my neighbour, and that he is therefore as good as I'.[25] Substantial inequalities are socially harmful, whether they are inequalities of resources or of power: 'The present exaggerated inequalities in the sharing of the products of industry lead to one-sided relationships of dependence, giving to some an arbitrary power over others, producing class antagonisms, leading to jealousy and hatred in the victims of arbitrary power, and to pride and contempt in those who wield it.'[26] Thus policies are advocated which will do away with substantial inequalities in wealth and power.

The call for a more equal ordering of society goes along with a comprehensive package of proposals which is markedly more specific than those in Temple's *Christianity and Social Order*. The exercise of economic power must be made responsible to the community through appropriate organs. The unfettered and irresponsible pursuit of private and group interests was clearly held to blame for much of the misery of the 1930s.[27] 'The common interest', the Commission declared, 'demands a far greater measure of public control of capital resources and means of production than our tradition has in the past envisaged'.[28] This control might mean common ownership, by the state, by public corporations, or by co-operatives; or it might be adequately exercised through government direction of a substantially increased sort. Certainly democratic planning was an absolute necessity. 'We have striven', said Baillie, 'to abide by the principles as to the limits of the Church's concern and competence which we have laid down for ourselves. We make no political recommendations. We discuss no economic theory. We confine ourselves to laying down certain prior conditions which must be observed by any political or economic programme, no matter by what "ism" it calls itself or does not call itself, to which Christians living in the present situation can give their assent. For instance, we say that "economic power must be made objectively responsible to the community as a whole"; but we do not attempt to say, because it is a matter to which the Christian revelation does not extend and on which the Church as such has therefore no right to speak, whether and to what extent this must involve the direct ownership by the State of the means of production and dis-tribution.'[29]

In matters of social policy the Commission gave considerable attention, as might have been expected, to education and among the values it wished to see reaffirmed and more fully expressed than previously was equality of educational opportunity.[30] Far less detailed consideration is given to social security, the maintenance of full employment, and the possibility of a National Health Service, although these things seem to follow from the Commission's concern for the stability of the family:

> To look for stability in the sexual life and conduct of young men and women is neither reasonable nor fair if it is next to impossible to secure houses which can be made into homes, or if there is no reasonable certainty of regular employment for the maintenance of home and family. All who believe that good homes are the foundation of the Church and the community are committed thereby to a practical policy which will secure the fullest possible extension of health services providing ante-natal care and advice, maternity homes on an adequate scale, and means for ensuring the welfare of mothers and young children. Communal services such as the provision of milk, school meals, and play-centres for

little children; the multiplying of nursery schools on an adequate scale; the development of school education and of after-school activities for adolescent youth in such a way that the educational institution co-operates with the home and shares its problems of training and discipline – all of these are the concern of the Church and call for the support and service of Christian people, because by the help of such means the home can be enabled to fulfil even better than at any time in the past its function as the training ground of the young. . . . One essential part of the fight is to secure universally those physical, material, and educational conditions under which true homes can come into existence.[31]

The tone is no doubt moralistic, and the welfare state which is sought is expected to conserve and uphold the traditional virtues of family life and personal morality. But this should not obscure two significant facts about the Baillie Commission. first, it envisaged and called for sweeping changes in British society because it held that a return to the pre-war situation was unthinkable and morally unacceptable; the War had shown other possibilities and aroused expectations which this time must not be disappointed. These changes were in the direction of an egalitarian welfare state: indeed the Commission was interested in the framing of a more equal and fraternal society rather than a society in which the most significant reform was simply the establishment of a floor below which no one would be allowed to fall, while above that level little would be changed. The second point to note about the Baillie Commission is that in contrast with Temple and Tawney's books, this was an official church commission whose reports were approved by the highest authorities in the church. In other words, the Baillie Commission indicated as substantial a degree of commitment as is possible for a denomination to a new pattern of social order. It played no small part in swinging public opinion, not only Christian opinion, in Scotland behind a model of post-war Britain as an egalitarian welfare state.

In short, the Commission mobilized a denomination, and much Christian opinion outside that denomination, behind fairly specific policies and proposals for legislation, and provided these proposals with a Christian and theological rationale.

4. Building a consensus

A proper account and assessment of the Christian contribution to the making of the welfare state in Britain has yet to be written.[32]

All we have attempted to do by way of a brief examination of Tawney, Temple and the Baillie Commission is to suggest that much Christian thinking was moving in the 30s and early 40s towards endorsement of the project of building a welfare state in post-war Britain. The Christian conscience had been touched by the destitution of the Depression and the hopes of the war period. Churchmen and theologians saw themselves as having a responsibility to contribute to the debate about the future shape of Britain and mobilize church opinion to support certain lines of social reform. There was not, of course, unanimity in the churches, in particular over the desirability of equality as a social ideal, an integral part of the welfare state package. Some influential churchmen saw welfare purely in terms of individual charity on the one hand, and a government-sponsored safety net on the other. An aristocrat like Lord Eustace Percy represented a paternalist tradition which rejected any idea of social engineering and advocated private charity supplemented by means-tested public provision for the poorest, in the older tradition of British social policy.[33] But such views were regarded as those of mavericks who did not accept the egalitarian Christian consensus.

One might, of course, suggest that in all this churchmen and theologians were simply reflecting 'advanced' secular opinion, and that the Christian consensus was no more than the counterpart or imitation of the growing popular desire for a welfare state in Britain. Such a view should not be rejected out of hand. There is some truth in it, but it is certainly lop-sided. While it may seldom be possible to trace specific Christian influence on policy there is little doubt that there was such an influence – take Temple's contribution to the 1944 Education Act as an example. And the churches managed to mobilize sectors of the population which were not predisposed to move in this direction into supporting the establishment of a welfare state. The churches were in the 1940s more socially comprehensive and politically influential than they are now, and they were able to mobilize wide support behind the idea that post-war Britain should be a compassionate and fraternal society in which equality found far fuller expression than it had in the past. The Christian position (if we may for the moment speak of such) was in pretty general terms. There was disagreement about the detailed objectives and some reticence about the strategy for achieving them. General support for a welfare society expressing broadly egalitarian ideals did not necessarily mean the endorsement of a welfare state, with central direction, nationalization, and socialism. But even when all necessary qualifications have been made, it remains true that there was in the 1940s a very considerable Christian contribution to the shaping and the support of the emerging welfare state in Britain, and a very considerable Christian investment in its success. In a real sense, Christianity provided the philosophy that the welfare state required.

It has often been suggested – most recently and forcefully by E. R. Norman – that Christian attitudes on social matters have usually in modern times been no more than reflections of secular opinions, disguised with a thin veneer of religiosity. We would argue, however, that the development of the welfare state was one of the rather few instances when Christian social thinking can be shown to have had a significant impact on the way things go in Britain. Without the efforts of Tawney and others to commend and translate into a secular idiom Christian social values, without the attempts of the ecumenical movement and William Temple to develop and use a responsible method of moving between Christian faith and policy options, without the successful mobilizing of Christian support by such bodies as the Baillie Commission, things would have been much different. This was also a major learning experience for the churches and for theology, about the nature and limits of Christian involvement in social, political and economic affairs. It would appear that many of these lessons have been forgotten today, and require to be relearned, with appropriate modifications for the new situation. But above all we should note that we have inherited a continuing responsibility for welfare provision as a matter which should not be separated from the Christian gospel.

5

The Collapse of
the Welfare Consensus

The welfare consensus, while it lasted, was a shared vision leading to shared social policies and giving the nation as a whole a sense of common purpose. In the 'Butskellite' era there was little difference in attitudes towards the welfare state between the two main parties, except that many people thought that the Tories on the whole ran the social services somewhat better. The euphoria of the welfare consensus meant that the two parties competed for the opportunity to be responsible for 'fine-tuning heaven'. The welfare state, like the monarchy or the Church of England, was assumed to be above politics; politicians might serve it, make it more effective, or tinker with details, but its fundamental desirability was for thirty years almost beyond question. It was assumed that there was a deep harmony between the welfare state and the mixed economy; that Keynesian economics had given techniques of economic management which could undergird the welfare state indefinitely; that major social problems such as poverty were either solved or well on the way to a solution; and that a quiet social revolution could be carried through without encountering strong and determined resistance from entrenched interests.

The cold winds of economic adversity awoke the sleeper and showed that the vision had been in large part a dream which bore little relation to the real world. In the 1970s the welfare state seemed to have become the pressure group state, a kind of arena for powerful interest groups to slog it out, forgetful of the position of the weak and the unorganized. Economic growth had salved social problems rather than solving them, and with the end of growth and the coming of harder times it became obvious that remedying social ills would be a costly business, hard to implement, and that there was precious little agreement about what the solutions might be. Confidence in the welfare state was shaken, and its legitimacy and indeed desirability in doubt. Even its most ardent supporters had to admit to a sense of disappointment that it had not achieved what they had hoped. And a new vigorous right-wing critique emerged which started from a thorough-going rejection of the welfare consensus and concluded that the welfare state should be stripped down and rebuilt on a fundamentally different basis.

The question of poverty was a central issue. If the welfare state meant anything at all, it was a society in which the giant Want had been put to flight or despatched for ever. During the consensus period most people believed that this was in fact the case. Prophets of the welfare state like R. H. Tawney declared that Britain had become a significantly more equal society and the great problems which had troubled the nation's conscience in the 1930s were well on the way to a solution. 'Clearly', he wrote in 1951, 'the time for self-congratulation has not yet come; but it is legitimate to feel a modest pride that a course in the right direction has been held by this country against the wind.'[1] But niggles of doubt soon began to appear; extensive poverty was, as it were, rediscovered; figures were produced to suggest that Britain was not, after all, becoming a more equal society; and it was argued that the new structures of the welfare state were in fact benefiting the prosperous far more than the needy.

The rediscovery of poverty was largely the work of three of Tawney's disciples, Brian Abel-Smith, Richard Titmuss, and Peter Townsend. In the 1940s and 50s there had been little academic interest shown in poverty in Britain. It was, apparently, assumed that the back of the problem had been broken, and what was left was tidying up and fringe arrangements. Abel-Smith and Townsend in their *The Poor and the Poorest* (1965) examined the incidence of poverty since the war. The poor were defined as those with an income below or slightly above the level of qualifying for National Assistance. They showed that there had been a significant increase between 1953 and 1960 both in the total number and in the proportion of the population living in poverty. They challenged the general complacency by showing that numbers of the poor and of the very poor had been growing steadily throughout the 1950s. Peter Townsend's massive and magisterial study, *Poverty in the United Kingdom* (1979) brought the picture up to date, with results which were even more alarming. His survey concluded that:

By the state's standard, there were 6.1 per cent of the sample in households, and 8.1 per cent in income units who, when their net disposable incomes were averaged over the previous twelve months, were found to be living in poverty. They represented 3,300,000 and 4,950,000 people respectively. A further 21.8 per cent in households and 23.2 per cent in income units were on the margins of poverty, representing 11,900,000 and 12,600,000 respectively. These measures were related to net disposable incomes for the twelve months prior to interview. By the state's own definition, therefore, there were between 15 and 17½ million in a population of some 55½ million who were in or near poverty.[2]

If poverty was not disappearing, but becoming steadily a more severe national problem, it was also true that welfare state Britain was not becoming a more equal society in incomes and wealth. There has been redistribution in Britain in the last fifty years, but recent studies are unanimous in suggesting that the movement has been from the very rich to the prosperous, rather than from the rich to the poor. The towering heights of personal wealth have been somewhat reduced for the benefit of the upper middle class, but this has had no positive impact whatever on the condition of the poor.[3] Besides, much of the redistribution had taken place before the welfare state was established.

The problem of poverty is also the problem of wealth, or rather the problem of the distribution of resources. Poverty is not an absolute standard of deprivation, the same in all cultures and ages; it is rather to be understood in the light of the standards regarded as acceptable in a particular context – that is the theory of 'relative deprivation'. Thus poverty is an expression, and a necessary expression, of inequality, and the two must be faced and tackled together. Poverty is inequality of the sort that denies fellowship. As David Donnison, who was for five years Chairman of the Supplementary Benefits Commission, put it, 'Poverty means a standard of living so low that it excludes people from the community in which they live', a definition elaborated in the Commission's Report for 1978:

To keep out of poverty, people must have an income which enables them to participate in the life of the community. They must be able, for example, to keep themselves reasonably fed, and well enough dressed to maintain their self-respect and to attend interviews for jobs with confidence. Their homes must be reasonably warm; their children should not feel shamed by the quality of their clothing; the family must be able to visit relatives, and give them something on their birthdays and at Christmas time; they must be able to read newspapers, and retain their television sets and their membership of trade unions and churches. And they must be able to live in a way which ensures, so far as possible, that public officials, doctors, teachers, landlords and others treat them with the courtesy due to every member of the community.[4]

Poverty is a network of deprivation and exclusion. The poor in economic terms are also poor in political resources, they are politically powerless, and they are pushed to the fringes of the community and increasingly concentrated in certain housing estates and areas of the inner cities where they are largely invisible to the more prosperous sections of the community. But the problem cannot be solved in isolation; it is an issue affecting the whole social structure.

What went wrong with the welfare state, which was intended to do just this, to cure poverty and make Britain a more equal community? One could answer this question in a detailed way, pointing to the gaps and failures in welfare provision for the poor: it is easy to demonstrate that means-tested benefits are not taken up by many who are entitled to them; short-term benefits are significantly lower than long-term benefits and by most standards are woefully inadequate; a high level of unemployment leads to much poverty, and the unemployed never get the higher level of benefit; there are serious gaps in relation to the long-term disabled, one parent families, etc. Some people sweepingly denounce the welfare state as itself a major cause of deprivation and poverty.[5] But for our present purposes we need simply to note the sense of disillusion engendered by the realization that something has gone wrong, that the welfare state has not delivered the goods, that problems such as poverty are still very much with us, and crying out for remedy.

1. The swing of opinion

With the breakdown of consensus there emerged a new political polarization, both vociferous extremes rejecting the middle ground and the New Right endeavouring to give the *coup de grace* to the old consensus and construct a new one on fresh foundations laid deep in the thought of Friedrich von Hayek and Milton Friedman. Increasing public disillusion with the welfare state powerfully encouraged this polarization, and in particular provided an opinion base and electoral support for the move to the right in British politics.

The swing of opinion is well documented by Peter Golding and Sue Middleton in their report on a survey of public attitudes towards welfare provision which is contained in their book *Images of Welfare*.[6] People in general felt that welfare benefits were too high and too easy to get. 59.5% of respondents agreed that 'The trouble with welfare benefits is it's too easy to get them'; among low wage earners this proportion is even higher (64.4%). A large majority found having to claim benefits shaming or embarrassing; there is still much stigma associated with claiming benefit. Nearly half of Golding and Middleton's sample believed that too much was being spent on welfare and social security, which was more than double the proportion who believed that more should be spent. A significant minority of 41.3% were suspicious of state welfare provision and thought that 'it would be better to pay low rates and taxes and let people pay for services as they want them'; most of these people were young or middle class. A survey by the New Right think tank, the Institute of Economic Affairs, conducted ten years previously found only a fifth to a quarter in favour of a policy which would 'take less in taxes, rates and national insurance, concentrate on people in need leaving others to pay or insure privately'. Support for this position was higher among the lower socio-economic groups.[7] Clearly support for welfare state provision is dwindling, and opposition or uneasiness is not limited to those who have high incomes and could most easily provide for themselves through the market by 'going private'. Although more than two thirds of respondents felt that the welfare state in Britain was something to feel proud of, a high proportion of them came from the lower income categories or were older, and four out of five believed that too many people were dependent on the welfare state, and seven out of ten believed that it made people lazy. 16.3% of respondents agreed with the statement that 'poor people have only themselves to blame, so there's no reason why society should support them'. In assessing overall attitudes to social security among their respondents, Golding and Middleton found that just over a third had high anti-welfare attitudes, and these tended to cluster among older people and manual workers. A considerable proportion regarded the unemployed as work-shy, and 11.7% believed the high level of unemployment benefits to be a cause of unemployment. Those out of work did not attract much sympathy, for it was commonly believed that much unemployment is voluntary, and involves little hardship; attitudes to the unemployed were sternest among the low paid. Little poverty is believed to exist; the poor are generally to blame for their own poverty; and they have become 'the spoilt darlings and cheats of the welfare state'. The welfare state appears to have generated more enemies than friends, and suspicion of it is spread right across the social spectrum. Even the idealistic folk who hoped that the welfare state would usher in a more fraternal form of society through eradicating poverty and carrying through significant measures of redistribution are disillusioned. It would not be too much to say that an anti-welfare state consensus is emerging, which blames the victims for their plight and smiles indulgently on wealthy tax evaders, while happily applauding, first, welfare retrenchment, and then the dismantling of the welfare state.

How has this come about? We have argued that the welfare consensus arose out of the experience of the Depression and the Second World War in particular. The anti-welfare consensus may be partly contrived and manipulated by the popular press and the media, but it also springs out of experience – the experience of inflated expectations disappointed by a remote and unintelligible bureaucratic system, by the contrast between the supermarket where the shopper is treated with respect and given freedom of choice because one person's money is as good as the next's, and the dowdy, impersonal social security office. The dream of a welfare society has for many become a nightmare of complexity and unfairness. The steady erosion of community feeling since the war has destroyed many of the solidarities on which the welfare state was founded, and was intended to strengthen. Jeremy Seabrook in his remarkable book, *What Went Wrong?*,[8] argues that capitalist and materialist values have been deeply corrosive of the sense of community which was at the heart of the hope for a welfare society. Everything must now be put in terms of money; money has the capacity to solve all problems; and as a result people fight one another to maintain differentials or increase their pay without concerning themselves with the search for a new and better society or with the lot of the underdog. It is a persuasive argument, and helps to explain the striking absence of enthusiasm for the welfare state, or indeed for social reform of any kind. The mood and the new consensus provide immense opportunities for the New Right, as Dexter Tiranti writes:

The New Right politicians make convincing sense of the world to many who have been puzzled, worried and intimidated by the changes of the last thirty-odd years. Their talent has been to sense the mood, articulate it and respond to it. Curiously for governments that so blatantly favour the rich and powerful, they are more in touch with ordinary people than politicians who have a more genuine claim to champion people's rights.[9]

But before we look in more detail at the New Right's attitude to welfare, we will examine the radicals' analysis of what went wrong.

2. The disenchantment of the Left

Two significant and complementary interpretations of what went wrong with the welfare state have recently appeared from the Left. Frank Field MP has argued that the patchwork generally labelled 'the welfare state', with its universalist and egalitarian thrust is only one part of statutory provision for the welfare of citizens; government also permits, provides or encourages other forms of supplying welfare to groups in the community which have powerful *and directly opposed* effects to those of the welfare state. These other 'welfare states' have effectively stultified the impact of the welfare state as it is commonly understood. And Julian Le Grand, an economist at the London School of Economics, has shown in detail how the major elements of the welfare state have not in any case had an equalizing impact: benefits have gone quite disproportionately to the already prosperous.

Frank Field has given us a salutary reminder that the state's involvement in matters of welfare is far more extensive than the measures arising out of Beveridge's proposals. In his book, *Inequality in Britain: Freedom, Welfare and the State*,[10] he describes four 'welfare states' in addition to the traditional welfare state based substantially on the work of Beveridge. These other 'welfare states', or ways the state provides for welfare, are: (1) 'The tax allowance welfare state', providing reductions in the tax liability of people in relation to specific circumstances, responsibilities and needs. Thus it makes a considerable and selective contribution to the welfare of these people – particularly those who have a good tax accountant who can wend his way through the jungle of tax legislation. (2) 'The company welfare state' is concerned with the benefits and additional provisions which companies increasingly provide for at least some of their employees – company pensions, sick benefits, medical insurance and the like, together with 'perks' such as company cars, entertainment allowances, company suits and so forth. These company benefits have considerably increased in recent years, and tend to favour the more highly paid employees, so that they represent in many cases a very considerable hidden addition to top salaries. Thus the impact of the company welfare state is to increase inequality, and sometimes, as in the case of private health insurance, it contributes to undercutting the universal provision as well. It counts as a welfare *state* because the state through its taxation provisions smiles on such arrangements and subsidizes them. (3) 'The unearned income welfare state': here inherited wealth continues to provide an income, or more usually a supplement to income, which is a benefit which enables its owner to have a higher standard of life. This form of wealth is most unequally distributed and there are a wide variety of legal ways of ensuring that it is passed on from generation to generation despite redistributive measures such as capital transfer tax. (4) 'The private market welfare state'. Particularly in health and education wealthier individuals and companies can opt out of the general provision and 'go private'. Both private education and private medicine are heavily subsidized by the state, e.g. through charitable status of schools giving tax exemption and through companies' corporate subscriptions to schemes such as BUPA being set against taxable income, thus reducing the nation's tax base.

Field's five 'welfare states', or rather elements in the state's commitment to welfare, need to be considered together to get a balanced impression of how welfare *actually* operates in Britain, who the beneficiaries are, and what the cumulative social impact is. It seems clear that all the four additional 'welfare states' to which Frank Field has so dramatically drawn our attention are radically inegalitarian in their effects. The benefits go overwhelmingly to those who are already powerful and prosperous, and probably do more than offset any equalizing impact of the 'Beveridge welfare state'. And this is no accident, nor a tribute to the foresightedness and sagacity of the beneficiaries, but a matter of legal endorsement of those four 'welfare states', an endorsement which carries with it the deployment of huge amounts of public money for the benefit of the prosperous through tax exemptions and allowances. The picture which emerges from Frank Field's book puts a quite different light on the dispute between those who believe in universal benefits and those who are selectivists. It appears that in the British multifaceted welfare state the universal benefits are dwarfed by the selective ones, and of the latter the vast preponderance goes, not to the needy, but to those who are already wealthy. As a whole, therefore, it can be said that the real welfare state is a congeries of ill-assorted and sometimes incompatible schemes, the total effect of which is certainly not to redistribute income in favour of the poor or build a more equal society in Britain.

Frank Field's four other 'welfare states' in principle and in practice are intended to provide mainly for the more prosperous; they encourage *inequality* and accordingly have much responsibility for the increase of poverty and the failure of the 'Beveridge' welfare state to produce what was expected of it. For far too long the attention of people interested in welfare, poverty and equality was directed almost exclusively to matters such as social security, education, housing and so forth, and only minimally to the other ways government provides welfare or encourages others to provide welfare for selected groups through the organization of the fiscal system. Now that the focus of attention has been widened[11] we can see clearly how strong are the tensions and oppositions within the total provision of welfare, and how effectively these contrary provisions have been in neutralizing or even reversing developments hoped for from the Beveridge proposals.

But even when we narrow our attention to the first of Frank Field's welfare states, there are major problems. It is a fair generalization that most of the Beveridge proposals were intended to benefit the whole community and particularly the poorest, the two objectives being seen as complementary. Brian Abel-Smith asked in 1958 who benefited from the welfare state. His answer was that the middle classes received a far better deal from the welfare state than did the poor, although the current mythology was that the welfare state was largely for the benefit of the poor. 'The middle classes', he argued, 'get the lion's share of the public social service, the elephant's share of occupational welfare privileges, and in addition can claim generous allowances to reduce their tax liability.'[12] Abel-Smith's paper was intended to counter middle class attacks on the welfare state as 'feather-bedding the poor' and providing hardly anything for other sectors of the community, but the clear implication of his argument is that the welfare state is neither curing poverty nor equalizing British society – indeed the suggestion is that it may be doing just the reverse.

In a recent book, *The Strategy of Equality* (the title is borrowed from one of the chapter headings in Tawney's *Equality*), Julian Le Grand asks whether the social services have in fact acted as agents of equalizing British society, as Tawney and others of the pioneers hoped they would. Le Grand is well aware that the social services are only part, but a not unimportant part, of Tawney's strategy. He examines in detail health, education, housing, and transport, and asks how in their operation they measure up against five criteria of equality: that there should be equal expenditure for each relevant individual; that there should be a redistribution of final income from rich to poor; that there should be equality of access; equal costs to everyone using the service; and equality of outcome. His conclusions are sombre:

> Overall, it is difficult to avoid the implication that the strategy of promoting equality through public expenditure in the social services has failed. It has failed to achieve full equality of whatever kind for most of the services reviewed. In those areas where data are available it has failed to achieve greater equality over time; and in some cases it is likely that there would be greater equality if there was no public expenditure on the service concerned.[13]

It is notable that Le Grand does not give any attention to social security, the personal social services, or taxation. But it is doubtful whether studies in these areas would lead him to modify his conclusion that the benefits of the welfare state go overwhelmingly to the better off, and it has at best a negligible equalizing impact. Abel-Smith's conjectures back in 1958 are even truer today.

This answer to the question of who benefits from the welfare state goes some way to explaining the strength of the consensus which existed until recently in support of the welfare state: it was backed by people who knew that it provided quite well for them and its supposed equalizing effects would not adversely affect their interests. There is no need to conjecture about a middle class conspiracy to subvert the strategy of equality. What is clear is that although the welfare state may have – certainly has – produced many good things, and is worth defending on this account, it has not fulfilled the expectations of those who saw it as primarily and centrally a technique of making Britain a more equal society. Perhaps it was naive to suppose that it should. Certainly precedents do not spring easily to mind where a radical social revolution has been carried through by a consensus almost painlessly, and without encountering serious political opposition. Tawney, we may remember, did not invest such hopes in the ability of the social services to effect a social revolution as have some of his disciples. He was aware that the strategy of equality had to have political and economic teeth, and that redistribution and other equalizing measures were sure to arouse opposition and could not be coated with sugar to make them acceptable to one and all. Piecemeal and indirect measures may be good in themselves, but they are hardly likely to be able to resist the strong and well deployed forces of inequality in British society. And sometimes measures have the opposite effect from that intended. For instance, it has been argued that universal provision for all without regard to need, while it avoids the stigma of a means test can mean that inequality is sustained or increased.[14] As Richard Titmuss put it, classless services are really impossible in a class-ridden society.[15] A strategy for equality has to be comprehensive. We cannot leave it to education alone, or to education and the other social services, to make Britain a more equal society. Only a comprehensive approach which takes politics seriously is capable of doing the job.

The hopes that the welfare state would be a key element in an effective strategy of equality and effect substantial redistribution of resources have been disappointed. Massive expenditure on the welfare state makes hardly any impact on economic inequality, and indeed may help to exacerbate it. The universality of provision, which is so central to the idea that the welfare state is to be midwife at the birth of a more equal welfare society rather than simply providing a safety net for the most unfortunate, has made equalizing through positive discrimination almost impossible, and certainly exceedingly costly. If one wants to achieve redistribution of resources, as egalitarians do, it is probably better to do it directly through fiscal arrangements rather than indirectly through welfare provisions. And redistribution meets strong opposition from various interests, including trade unions which have shown themselves more reluctant to allow the 'social wage' to moderate demands for cash in the pocket, or to encourage the state to redistribute resources to pensioners, the unemployed and the poorest at the expense of their members' wage packets.[16] The expectation that the welfare state, on its own and relatively painlessly, might effect radical egalitarian social change has not been fulfilled. Too little attention has been paid to other agencies of change, to a comprehensive approach, and to the politics of equality. The strength and pervasiveness of structures of inequality has been consistently underestimated, and very little has been done to counter the ideology of inequality, what in earlier generations was known as the 'religion of inequality'. The welfare state, the radicals conclude, should be rethought, and then reformed as part of a comprehensive plan for moving towards a more equal welfare society. But its objectives and basic principles are pronounced sound; it is the details which require attention.

Such critiques of the welfare state stand within the Fabian, gradualist and moderate tradition. There is a strong moral emphasis, to which many Christians must be sympathetic. But the theory on which the critiques are based is not rigorously developed and represents little advance on the consensual thinking of the 1940s. It has difficulty in coping with and responding vigorously to the more hard-headed ideologically-based questionings of the radical Left and the radical Right. The radical Left sees the welfare state as representing a temporary equilibrium between capital and labour which performs a set of conflicting functions: it serves to obscure the developing contradictions of capitalism and recruit popular support for capitalism. It involves no fundamental change in the capitalist system, but is a cosmetic improvement of the image of capitalism. Hence it may operate to delay necessary and radical social change, but it also debilitates the capitalist system in the long run by diverting resources from production to welfare and imposing limits on the freedom of the market – points also made by the radical Right. There is no basic incompatibility between capitalism and the welfare state; indeed it is regarded as a necessary prop to the system and a subtle form of social control. But for all that, the New Left is thoroughly ambivalent in its attitude to the welfare state. It is to be defended against attacks from the Right: welfare is cut back when it is felt no longer to serve the needs of capital, or an opportunity occurs to weaken labour. But many of the criticisms echo points made from the radical Right, and left-wing thinkers in some moods can suggest that the kind of change they seek would only be possible as a popular reaction against a pure capitalism denuded of the welfare sugar-coating. What both the radical Left and the radical Right offer is structural, rather than pragmatic and moral, analyses and explanations of what is happening to the welfare state. But the ideology and the proposals of the radical Left have surprisingly little impact and little appeal in today's Britain, unlike those of the radical Right, to which we now turn.

3. The New Right: breaking the spell of the welfare state?

When the Central Policy Review Staff's paper on possible cuts in public expenditure was leaked to the press in September 1982, there were immediate cries of outrage from all quarters. It was then formally repudiated by the Prime Minister in such a way as to suggest that the proposals had been shelved, but might well be heard of again. In education the paper suggested the ending of state funding for all institutions of higher education, and substantial savings in primary and secondary education by allowing the staff: pupil ratio to rise. The idea of vouchers for education was considered. It would not lead to savings – indeed it might even increase expenditure – but it is advocated by many leading right-wingers on ideological grounds. What it would probably effect is an increase in the private educational sector at the expense of the public sector, especially if the latter continues to be starved of necessary resources. Substantial savings are advocated in social security by holding down all benefits below the level of inflation. And the National Health Service could be replaced by a system of private health insurance similar to that in operation in the United States. These proposals would result in large savings, but the Think Tank is clear, and justly so, that this would almost certainly operate to the disadvantage of the poor.[17] Such policies would involve the demolition of the welfare state. Yet it cannot but be noticed that in essence they are simply the acceleration of present policies. And they rest on a positive and emphatic repudiation of the welfare state as we know it, which is derived from the resurgent ideology of the New Right.

The outrage at these and other similar proposals is not hard to understand. But no one should have been surprised at them, especially if they were familiar with the publications of the influential Institute of Economic Affairs, the think-tank of the New Right, with racy titles like, *Wither the Welfare State* (1981), *Over-ruled on Welfare* (1979), and *Breaking the Spell of the Welfare State*, with their heady mix of swashbuckling rhetoric, dubious research and dogmatic generalizations. The welfare state is seen as the 'nanny state' which raises fundamental moral issues 'by reducing adults to the status of children who are left with pocket money rather than being trusted with responsibility for managing their own incomes'.[18] A vast bureaucracy peddles increasingly inferior goods, and feathers its own nest in the process. It weakens the family and all voluntary forms of self-help and its efforts to deal with distress more often than not increase distress. It puts equality before liberty, and can only be sustained by coercion. But through a kind of historical inevitability the welfare state is already withering away, and sound government policy will allow it to die and be replaced by market provision. As Arthur Seldon writes:

> The day-to-day reality of the welfare state has been 'compassion' concealing power-seeking, selflessness as a cloak for self-interest, God inscribed on the banner of Mammon. The reality is

concealed mistreatment of the aged, open strikes against children in hospital, the cutting of school lunches rather than superfluous staff. . . . The purpose of the welfare state in day-to-day reality has changed from the prevention of inadequacy to the pretence of equality. And since the effort to create and enforce equality – however unsuccessful – requires the suppression of differences, the welfare state has come into conflict with the free society. The British welfare state has logically and ineluctably become the main instrument in the creation of equality by coercion.[19]

Ralph Harris sums up:

What the electorate must teach the paternalistic politicians is that the 'welfare state' is anything but a gift horse. Rather it is a lame nag harnessed to an outdated bandwagon. So far from being duly grateful for being taken for a ride, the sovereign people should pull hard on the reins, ask for their money back and get off the overcrowded monstrosity.[20]

Right-wing attitudes to the welfare state cover a wide range, but it is now the more negative views which are dominant, and behind these there lurk the theories of F. von Hayek, Milton Friedman and R. Nozick. On one wing there is an aristocratic, paternalistic conviction that it is a proper responsibility of the state to provide for the needy. Friedman is right to note that there is no necessary connection between socialism and the welfare state, and that Bismark's patrician German Empire was one of the first attempts to produce something like a welfare state.[21] The idea that the state has some responsibility for charity and the welfare of its citizens has proved attractive to some conservative Christian thinkers: 'It is clear,' writes Professor Brian Griffiths, 'that government has an important role to play in this area'.[22] But there is disagreement as to the extent of the state's role, some right wingers accepting the outlines of the present welfare state in Britain, some seeing the need for a balance between statutory and voluntary provision, and some advocating a 'long-stop' role for the state, whereby only those of the needy who have failed to receive assistance in any other way may fall back on the state. But the point where almost all people of right wing views are agreed is that welfare and social engineering are different things; the state's responsibilities in the field of welfare have nothing whatever to do with redistributing resources to make a more equal society. Welfare is seen as assisting the victims of circumstances, but has nothing to do with challenging or changing the circumstances which lead to deprivation or altering the social or economic orders. Griffith's view is typical of right-wing opinion, tempered by Christian conviction: it is, he suggests, rather immoral that 'the modern welfare state is interested not so much in relieving poverty as redistributing income to achieve a more egalitarian distribution'; state action to relieve poverty is desirable, but only as a supplement to private and voluntary charity'.[23]

Right-wing thinkers, then, on the whole accept the desirability of *some* state provision for welfare. Most of them want to reduce the state's role and encourage voluntary and market provision, and almost all wish to treat welfare issues, particularly poverty, in isolation from questions of social change. Poverty and inequality, they suggest, are two different issues which have been falsely compounded by those who, by defining poverty in terms of relative deprivation, see poverty as inequality, or as a symptom of the disease of inequality.

The right-wing analysis of the present welfare state starts with a significant overlap with the radical critique: the welfare state favours the middle classes rather than the poor. The clearest instance of this is higher education. As Milton Friedman points out, most students are from middle or upper class backgrounds, and most of them are likely with their educational qualifications to earn high salaries, yet their education is highly subsidized from taxation, thus redistributing income from the poorer to the richer.[24] The redistributional effect is the opposite of that intended, resources are being diverted from the needy to the more prosperous, and people who have no need of help are receiving it. Welfare should not be used for inducing social change; its function is meeting human need; and the two aims are, Friedman believes, incompatible with one another. Welfare has even shown itself to be a counter-productive instrument of social change. In the second place, the welfare state is massively expensive, and often the expense is out of all proportion to the quality of the service provided. The near monopoly of the state in the provision of welfare removes important limits to an uncontrolled growth in costs. Much of the expenditure is swallowed up by elephantine bureaucracies, so that a significant part of the answer to the question of who benefits from the welfare state is: the rapidly increasing army of people who administer and provide the services. This again serves to blunt any redistributional effect, for the bureaucracy takes a slice of the resources as they pass through the system, and it also tends to make the service cumbrous and inefficient. The services may often be unsatisfactory, but improvement or alternative arrangements are strongly resisted by the powerful vested interests of the bureaucrats and providers of the services on the one hand and the recipients, beneficiaries and clients on the other. The more swashbuckling critics, like Rhodes Boyson, denounce the welfare state as morally enervating: paternalism (for that is how they see it) weakens 'the moral fibre of our people' by doing for them things they had better do for themselves. People are featherbedded, and become irresponsible, infantile and dependent. Their freedom is infringed, not yet to the extent that it is in a totalitarian state, but by denying them the right to take risks and make choices.[25]

The alternative is to pare down the welfare state to something we can afford. But even in more prosperous times it would still be desirable to reduce the state's provision of welfare to a safety net for the most unfortunate and encourage the development of voluntary charity. Hayek advocates the maintenance of a minimum income by the state, which is a kind of welfare 'floor'; Friedman has advocated a negative income tax, whereby those below the poverty line – defined absolutely not relatively – will receive supplementary income through the fiscal system rather than paying income tax.[26] Beyond this provision for the relief of absolute poverty, neither taxation nor the welfare services are really to be concerned with redistribution on a large scale, or with changing the face of society. The only long-term answer to the problem of poverty lies in sustained economic growth; 'a rising tide lifts all boats', as J. F. Kennedy said. But economic growth, according to Hayek and others depends on continuing inequality.[27] Because it has some responsibility for sustaining the conditions in which economic growth is encouraged – for Hayek government is like the maintenance department in a factory: it is necessary, but it doesn't actually produce anything – the state can make its proper contribution to the elimination of poverty and the common welfare. But the direct interventions of the welfare state have clearly failed and government should retire as quickly as possible to its referee role of setting and enforcing the rules rather than playing the game. Milton Friedman realizes that government cannot abolish the welfare state overnight; a transitional arrangement is necessary

> that could enhance individual responsiblity, end the present division of the nation into two classes, reduce both government spending and the present massive bureaucracy, and at the same time, assure a safety net for every person in the country, so that no one need suffer dire distress.[28]

After the transition, the place of the various welfare services would be taken by market provision in most cases. In relation to medicine and education, for instance, it is argued that collective provision is both less efficient and has lower standards than private provision in which there is no monopoly but the supply is regulated by market forces. Both these points deserve close scrutiny, as does the other belief that such a change would increase the freedom of everyone by extending choice. It is certainly doubtful whether it would increase the freedom of those who are already underprivileged.[29] Indeed it is likely that it would lead to a reduction in the freedom of the majority of people.

The resultant policies are, in effect, nothing but a dismantling of the welfare state and its replacement with what existed before. It neglects the sense of guilt, outrage and horror which that earlier situation aroused in morally sensitive people's minds, and the abundant evidence that laissez faire capitalism, while it may lead to considerable economic growth does not provide morally acceptable solutions to the problem of distribution, and did not provide either liberty or an adequate level of welfare for a large section of the population. The solution that Hayek, Friedman, Keith Joseph and their ilk propose has already been tried and found wanting. The nineteenth century was not an idyllic period of great prosperity for many people in Britain. This solution seems to neglect the lessons of history.

Disappointment and disillusion with the welfare state is concentrated particularly at the two extreme poles of political view. The extreme left is depressed that the welfare state has not served to bring a new society to birth. Equality has not been achieved, nor poverty eliminated. The welfare state has failed as a strategy for thorough-going social change. It was presented as a way of 'giant-killing'; but the giants continue to flourish. The radical right attributes the deficiencies of the welfare state to its holistic approach: instead of seeking to solve the more glaring social problems one by one, the welfare state operated on the premise that things were connected, and that lasting solutions to social problems depended on tackling the problems at their roots, in the way society was organized and run. The project was in fact more revolutionary and more utopian than Beveridge and others of its progenitors recognized. But the problems so boldly attacked have not been put to flight. The acceptance of public responsibility for the most disadvantaged has mushroomed into a vast and incredibly expensive, as well as ineffective, programme of social change. In hard times, they say, the country simply cannot afford to continue this vast degree of public expenditure for the achievement of objectives some of which, like equality, are regarded as questionable.

There is also a range of middle positions. Many people, of various political persuasions, are willing to recognize the considerable achievements of the British welfare state. The National Health Service is certainly capable of improvement and suffers from an unwieldy bureaucracy, but it provides a remarkably high quality of health care for almost everyone in the country. Comprehensive education was born and nurtured in controversy, but seems gradually to be demonstrating its worth, judged by any appropriate criterion – and this is an instance of a policy which is emphatically egalitarian. The social security system, for all its deficiencies, has transformed the state's provision for the needy. And one could go on to develop a lengthy panygyric for the welfare state as it is, warts and all, which would command the assent of many reasonable and informed people of all parties. The people in the middle ground would then go on to speak of disappointments and criticisms. Many of them relate to the role of the state: government plays too great a role in welfare; the welfare state has not encouraged the growth of a welfare society as it should; there is too much dependence engendered; and so on.

Differing analyses lead to differing solutions and programmes. The extreme left may see the whole apparatus of the welfare state as palliative rather than therapeutic, a lubricant to the system which itself engenders social problems. They see helping people in need as good only when it is a means to the new society, and often have a touchingly naive conviction that 'the revolution' will solve everything as if by magic. The radical right welcomes what has been described as 'the withering away of the welfare state',[30] and resolves to accelerate the process, running down the existing system of public provision for welfare until it is little more than a safety net; and private and voluntary agencies come in to fill the gap with market provision of services.

Widespread popular disenchantment with the welfare state backed by hard argumentation derived from the philosophy of possessive individualism have set the scene for a possible thorough-going reorganization of welfare which would also be a radical recasting of the moral basis of British society. This sets the agenda for the most important debate about the future shape of British society since the early 1940s.

6

The Public Role
of the Church Today

Of recent studies on the 'state of the nation' three stand out as
particularly illuminating, perceptive and well-informed: Ralf
Dahrendorf's *On Britain* (1982), A. H. Halsey's Reith Lectures,
Change in British Society (1978), and Anthony Sampson's *The
Changing Anatomy of Britain* (1982). The authors are careful
observers and present convincing accounts of contemporary Britain. None of them sees any need to discuss the place of the churches
or of Christianity in modern Britain. Sampson adorns his end
papers with a diagram of interlocking circles clustered around the
monarchy, signifying the major elements in his portrait of Britain –
the political parties, the press, industry, the universities, the armed
forces, local government, the schools, the police, and so on. The
churches do not appear in the diagram, and in the book there is only
one reference to the churches – in a discussion of devolution,
interestingly enough – and a strange little apology in the Introduction which betrays both a rather narrow understanding of the
churches' role, and perhaps a trifle of uneasiness about it: the book
is not 'about the spiritual side of the British, or questions of private
or public morality: I have not attemped to write about the churches,
which have influenced many other areas of power'.[1]

These books are a symptom of the times, with their underlying
assumption that the churches and the Christian faith have minimal
impact on British institutions and 'the way things go' in Britain. The
churches are not seen as a significant organ in the anatomy of
Britain and it is not necessary to ask questions about the churches if
one is to understand contemporary Britain. They are peripheral and
can easily be disregarded as a kind of side-show while the real

business is conducted elsewhere in total independence of the churches' views and reactions. It is doubtful whether books on such themes could have been written in the 1930s and 40s which neglected the place of the churches so blandly. For in the intervening decades there have been massive social changes in Britain which have effectively relegated the churches to the margins, undercut the once general belief that the churches are among the major institutions of society, and almost destroyed the expectation that the churches can and should be constructively engaged with matters of public policy and the shape of British society. Depleted and often nervous churches, uncertain of their role and evoking a confused image in the public mind of what they are there for, face a radically new situation in society, fresh problems and new issues. The old responses regurgitated just will not do. For the position of the churches has changed, and changed radically; and the issues presented by society are different too. A constructive response to the issues of today – most notably the question of the future of welfare – demands first taking the measure of the changed position of the churches, with the problems and opportunities which flow from this; and then engaging with the question of constructive involvement in the debate about welfare. In this chapter we will sketch the changed position of the churches, and some of the responses open to them.

The processes sometimes rather loosely lumped together and labelled secularization have their roots in the more distant past, but have undoubtedly been powerfully operative in the last thirty years. All statistics of religious observance have shown a sharp and steady decline since 1956. There are interesting variations in the figures geographically, in relation to different sects and denominations, and in different forms of observance. Scotland has significantly higher rates of church attendance than the south of England, for example, but in both contexts the curve goes steadily downwards and it seems probable that we are dealing here with a time-lag rather than any more substantial difference. The Roman Catholics and some of the smaller sects have markedly better rates of attendance than do the mainline Protestant churches – differences which can be explained in various ways, but do not offset the fact that the over-arching tendency is in decline. People cling on to certain rites of passage long after they have abandoned other forms of religious observance. Otherwise unchurched people still look for a Christian funeral and, to a lesser degree, a church wedding and baptism for their children. Figures in a matter such as this are not, of course, easy to interpret. There is certainly more of a diffuse and vaguely Christian religiosity around than the figures for religious practice might suggest. But the churches as institutions have very many fewer people participating in their activities, a far smaller proportion of the population on their books, and markedly fewer clergy than they had thirty years ago. There are, of course, vast numbers of people who never darken a church door but like to have the church there to stay away from, people whose names do not appear on church rolls but have a tenacious sense of belonging which deserves recognition, and a diffuse expectation that the church should 'do something' or 'say something'. They often object very vehemently when the church *does* say or do anything specific, if it comes to their ken!

Numerical decline has been closely associated with decline in influence. This is not to say that the reduction in numbers is the sole and adequate cause for the decline of influence. One could argue that there has been a major failure of nerve on the part of the churches, a nostalgic reluctance to admit the possibility that (to use Mrs Thatcher's language) a 'leaner, fitter' church might be more, rather than less, effective in its social witness. The fact that it no longer commands such big battalions could well be one reason why the churches are taken less seriously than once they were by the powerful in Britain, but there are other reasons as well. The consensus years were a time when Daniel Bell and many others proclaimed the end of ideology, and the term 'theology' became a rude word applied to any kind of theorizing or engagement with matters of principle which did not have an immediate applicability. With the end of consensus and the emergence of the New Right in Britain, Thatcherism was labelled by its opponents 'theological', doctrinaire or dogmatic. Theology has certainly had a bad press! In the consensus years the general tendency was to give a warm but very unspecific theological endorsement to the consensus; in the more abrasive intellectual atmosphere of today the theology which gave its benediction to consensus finds it hard to put on the boxing gloves, and enter the ring when the real hard-hitting ideological fight begins. Whatever the reasons may be – and they are undoubtedly many and various – there is no doubt that the churches in Britain have lost much influence in the last thirty years. They no longer have an almost guaranteed access to the corridors of power, a right to represent their views on a whole range of public issues; they now have to *win* the right to be heard by the insight, relevance and cogency of their positions.

The ending of the old consensus has served to underline the fact that Britain is a plural society, in which a rich diversity of racial groups, religions, political, ethical and social opinions, and more general world views exist side by side. The phenomenon of pluralism, as Peter Berger points out, is closely associated with secularization. Pluralism, like secularization, is sometimes embraced by Christians as a source of enrichment – a plural society is more open, exhilarating, fertile and creative than a more monochrome form of community, or so the argument runs. A totalitarian society depends on the successful enforcement of one orthodoxy, of one set of values, of one world-view; a kind of compulsory consensus lies at the foundation of totalitarian social order, legitimating it and defining it over against other, more open societies. Even Christendom fitted this pattern: Jews, Albigensians and other 'deviants' had to be excluded or suppressed to maintain the ideological unity of the society. A plural society, on the other hand, is open to a multiplicity of views, values and opinions. It enforces little by the way of explicit ideology, although to be sure there has to be a high level of acceptance of the value of tolerance, openness, etc. This 'secular Anglicanism' has its value; John Habgood argues that 'it shows tolerance and resilience verging on complacency; it is the expression of British adaptability and pragmatism. Though under threat from some of the growing divisions in British society, it succeeded in carrying the country through the disruptions of the 1960s and the more recent "winters of discontent" without fatal damage to the fundamentally humane tradition of public life'.[2] One might suggest, as Habgood does, that 'secular Anglicanism' has roots in not-so-secular Anglicanism but this may be no more than the assertion, true but perhaps not very important, that this, like so much else in a secular society such as Britain, is historically part of the detritus of a Christian past. Certainly it is not enough to allow us to continue to speak of Britain as a Christian country. But the more important question is how much agreement on values and general understanding of the world is required for a healthy, open and plural society. Durkheim saw religion as performing a vital role in social cohesion, and even avowedly atheist societies such as the Soviet Union find they have to manufacture elaborate surrogates for religion. British society too has been fertile in producing substitute religions and quasi-religions, but few if any of them seem capable of providing that resilient sense of common purpose which even at a time of crisis is capable of holding a community together without destroying freedom, and encouraging caring and fraternal relationships. It is a fundamental thesis of this book that the Christian church has a continuing responsibility, drawing on the riches of its tradition, to commend social values capable of acting as a basis for a healthy plural society, and that it can do this without advocating a retreat from pluralism in the direction of a revived Christendom.

Between them secularization and pluralism have left the churches still part of 'the system', and to some extent compromised by that fact. Certainly they do not have the freedom of manoeuvre that they sometimes dream of, because they are so deeply embedded in the broader society. Most of the British churches are in a kind of 'bourgeois captivity' which limits their vision and inhibits their ability to communicate with the poor. This, combined with institutional decline adds up to a confusing scene which can easily cause failure of nerve, or a kind of ecclesiastical identity crisis. It is clear that the old-style leadership and the old-style initiatives are no longer viable. But the new situation presents new opportunities, if only the churches can identify and grasp them.

The confident convictions of the New Right burst rudely upon the uncertainties and relativism generated by secularism and pluralism. When Mrs Thatcher entered Number Ten Downing Street for the first time as Prime Minister she chose to recite the prayer attributed to St Francis, apparently as a kind of slogan for her government, asking to be made an instrument of peace, bringing pardon where there was injury, hope where there had been despair, faith where there had been doubt and forgiveness where there had been offence. It reminded the more cynical of George Orwell's remark: 'An army of unemployed led by millionaires quoting the Sermon on the Mount – that is our danger'.[3] Mrs Thatcher's populist doctrine is one which systematically benefits the rich and soaks the poor. It conflicts at major points with the main thrust of Christian social teaching. But for various reasons, including the confidence with which it is affirmed, and the constant and misleading reiteration that 'There Is No Alternative', it has wide popular appeal.

Mrs Thatcher and some of her colleagues make strenuous attempts to ground their political views in Christian faith. She describes herself as a 'conviction politician', and frequently and publicly relates her faith to her political ideology and conduct of affairs. The Victorian and British values which she advocates are essentially Christian she asserts:

As we emerged from the twilight of medieval times . . . so we became what one historian has described as 'the people of a book and that book was the Bible'. . . . This people adopted, albeit gradually, a system of government and a way of living together which reflected the values implicit in that book. We acknowledged as a nation that God was the source of our strength and that the teachings of Christ applied to our national as well as our personal life.[4]

Christianity gives us the values we need for both private and public life, but that is not to say that Christianity prescribes one and only one course of action in politics. She puts much emphasis on the doctrine of sin, and on the consequences of human imperfectibility, which put a realistic limit to the possibilities of political action. In a sinful, fallen world, man remains a moral being, and must be given the freedom to choose – a theme which is a very central motif not only of Thatcherite philosophy, but of its policies as well. There is a very strong stress on individual responsibility, which is asserted to be Christian but emerges in a form more reminiscent of Samuel Smiles. And the regeneration of the individual is generally seen as prior to the renewal of society – an individualism which in practice is combined with centralized and authoritarian government.

One of the oddities of recent British history is that Mrs Thatcher and her colleagues and supporters have shown far more interest in church affairs, and devoted far more energy to attacking the churches than any other government for many decades. When the social responsibility secretaries of the major denominations signed a letter to *The Times* before the 1980 Budget, calling for a significant increase in Child Benefit for the million and a half families living below the poverty line, Patrick Jenkin, at that time the Secretary of State for Social Services, publicly rebuked the churches for illegitimate interference in matters of policy. The churches' remit, it was implied, concerned the salvation of individuals and the commendation of general values; beyond that it should not venture lest it get totally out of its depth. In pushing through the Nationality Act the Government found itself facing almost solid opposition from British church leaders. And similarly on issues of development and aid. The table of contents of a book published in 1984 by the Society for Promoting of Christian Knowledge but sponsored by the (New Right) Social Affairs Unit, *The Kindness that Kills: The Churches' Simplistic Response to Complex Social Issues*, reads like a catalogue of the points of issue between Thatcherism and the churches: wealth

67

creation, the role of multinational companies, attitudes towards South Africa, development aid, racism and the police, the closed shop, unemployment, education cuts, and the future of welfare. But the most significant area of tension is one not mentioned in this book: nuclear deterrence policy. And it was this last which led to a massive mobilization of Conservative Christian opinion to oppose the report of a Working Party of the Church of England Board for Social Responsibility entitled *The Church and the Bomb*. Ronald Butt wrote in *The Times* at that time:

> There is a sense in which prominent church figures who would not regard themselves as at all committed to party are nevertheless impaled on attitudes towards a whole range of contemporary questions, from defence to the economy, which make them instinctively hostile to the policies of the present Government.[5]

Indeed the situation was so disturbing to the Conservative Party that a conference was arranged by a group of Conservative MPs in early 1983 to affirm that it is possible to be a Christian and a Conservative! 'We want people to wake up to the fact that there are Christians in the Conservative Party', said an assistant director at Conservative Central Office.

All this was more than a little disconcerting for a party aware that it had for long been the Church Party, and whose leader claimed to base her policies on Christian premises and called for a return to traditional, and by implication Christian, virtues. Thatcherism sees itself, in contrast to all other contemporary British political ideologies, as being in need of ecclesiastical and theological support. The church as an institution plays a large role in its vision of the future of British society and the Thatcherite Conservative Party has shown more interest in church affairs and reacted more vigorously to church statements on political and economic issues than any other government since the war. But Thatcherism is profoundly uneasy about the line taken by the churches and suspicious of the present church leaders, with a few notable exceptions. One response to this situation, best exemplified in E. R. Norman's Reith Lectures, later published as *Christianity and World Order*, is to make a populist appeal direct to the rank-and-file of the churches, suggesting that their leaders are blind guides who have distorted the faith by politicizing it; they have reduced Christianity to a political programme and lost their grip on the central reality of faith which is, Norman believes, that Christianity is primarily concerned with 'the ethereal qualities of immorality' (the misprint in the last word appeared in *The Listener*'s version of the lectures). Assertions that Christianity is 'really' a spiritual and private matter, attacks on the 'politicization' of the faith, and appeals to the pew against the pulpit are all part of the stock-in-trade of Thatcherism today. The *idea* of the church bulks large in their view of things, but they are distinctly unhappy with the *reality* of the church which is so constantly questioning Government policy and raising awkward issues.

In such a situation there are three main possibilities before the churches. The first is to go through the door so invitingly held ajar by the New Right into the room, which turns out to be a cage, labelled 'private and domestic life'. Religion is to concern itself with the individual and his salvation, and with family life; it inculcates virtues and qualities of character which include a reverence for duly constituted authority and respect for the 'structure of things'. The withdrawal from the public realm is however, only apparently total: in fact this kind of privatized religion powerfully legitimates the activities of the powers that be, and encourages attitudes and patterns of behaviour which are essential for the smooth working of the system. The churches are seen as properly concerned with morality; indeed they should co-operate with government in maintaining personal and family values, leaving the market and the polity as autonomous systems which should be permitted to follow their own rules without ecclesiastical interference. Thatcherites are happy, however, when the churches produce men and women of character and drive to participate in public life. This sharp cleavage between the public and the private realms has, of course, a long history. The German Roman Catholic theologian Metz traces the privatization of Christianity back to the Enlightenment; others argue that Martin Luther's doctrine of the Two Kingdoms already encouraged the Christian evacuation of the public realm. But whatever its origins, privatization of Christianity confines the faith within a ghetto of cultic, moral and private irrelevance which, like most ghettoes, is seductive because it appears to be secure. That so much church life is already more or less comfortably ensconced in the private realm should not blind us to the fact that a private gospel is an incomplete gospel or make us forget that from the beginning the church has believed that it has a word to deliver to the public realm.

The second possibility is for the churches to cling on to the vestiges of establishment as if they were essential for the public relevance of the gospel. When Tony Benn, in March 1983, called for the disestablishment of the Church of England, he argued that even the contemporary modified form of legal establishment restricted the liberty of the church and made it subservient to the state. An established church, he argued, was compromised, and it was hardly possible for it to speak and act in a prophetic way. Church leaders with hopes of preferment would be unlikely to launch sustained attacks on the injustices of the powerful while government continued to have a say in church appointments. The Church of England needed to be freed from its 'subservience to the state' if it were to sustain its integrity as a Christian church. Benn's words aroused remarkably little controversy. One reason for this lack of interest was identified by Benn himself: 'We have grown so accustomed to these arrangements that their manifest absurdities and dangers are hardly noticed and rarely discussed in public.' Another might be the narrowness of his focus – instead of criticizing the whole complex and confusing series of linkages between the churches and the authorities in society, he chose to direct his fire at the legal establishment of the Church of England, which has so much of the Gilbert and Sullivan about it that many people just cannot see that substantial theological issues are involved in its continuance or termination. But these issues arise from the whole shape of the present relationship between the churches and the corridors of power rather than from the largely ceremonial area on which Tony Benn chose to concentrate.

If a left-winger like Tony Benn attempts, unsuccessfully, to spark off a campaign for disestablishment, right-wing thinkers like Roger Scruton are quite clear that the church is, and must remain, a major component of the 'Establishment'. A state, he argues, requires a myth the function of which is to point beyond the empirical realities of power and authority to some transcendent ground. The myth legitimates the exercise of power by placing it in the frame of the numinous, and elicits from the subjects a more profound quality of allegiance and patriotism. In Europe the ruling idea of establishment is the idea of a Christian society. Christianity, in other words, is *the* myth of European societies. This link between myth and power is consistently emphasized in conservative thought; conservatives believe in the idea of a Christian society whether, like T. S. Eliot or Lord Hailsham they believe and practise the Christian faith, or, like Burke and Disraeli, have a more distant and ambiguous relation to the church. Even conservatives who do not believe in God hold that this belief is important for politics, and particularly for the nurturing of a conservative disposition among

70

the people. 'It is the possession of that belief', Scruton writes, 'which enables men to direct their most powerful dissatisfactions away from the ruinous hope of changing things, to a more peaceable hope of being one day redeemed from the need to do so'.[6] Belief in a transcendent Being strengthens social bonds and helps to reconcile people to the present order of things. Conservatism can survive the demise of explicit religious commitments, but it always benefits from clear religious belief, widely diffused throughout the society. And the greatest danger to conservatism in a secular age is 'the transfer of frustrated religious feeling to petty secular causes'.[7]

In a European society, the church 'continues to provide the major institutions which reinforce the attachment of the citizen to the forms of civil life, and which turn his attention away from himself as individual, towards himself as social being'.[8] Whether or not *a* church is legally established, the church provides the binding principle for the other institutions of society and effectively attaches the citizen in loyalty to the commonwealth. The church must be politically central: 'the place of the church is either at the heart of things, or nowhere'.[9] But, Scruton believes, the leadership of the church 'has begun to set itself against the order of European society' and forfeited its spiritual authority by denying its essentially conservative role of supplying legitimation to the social order and consolation to the victims. Instead the church has become politicized while losing interest in the transcendent grounding of politics; and as the church loses the allegiance of the people who now seek elsewhere for religious fulfilment it becomes progressively too weak to sustain its primordial political role. Not disestablishment, but restoration of the church to its traditional centrality and its ancient priorities should be high on the agenda of Conservatives.

Roger Scruton's argument helps us to put the present Conservative Party's intense interest in church affairs into context and understand more adequately its significance. For many Christians there may be a seductive quality about his thought. We all believe, do we not, with Scruton, that the church should be at the heart of things, that Christianity is a public matter, that religion *matters*. It is flattering to find a philosopher taking the church so seriously; it is a long time since British philosophers and political theorists have devoted attention to the church. But a close reading of Scruton shows that he is affirming the church as a central institution of civil religion, and is not very interested in its Christian integrity; indeed he is positively antagonistic to an understanding of the church as an ecumenical and prophetic body, and uneasy about those elements of the Christian faith which make it such a poor civil religion. Machiavelli long ago recognized the indispensibility of religion for the strength of a political regime, and believed that only religion could effectively inculcate the civic virtues, effect ideological control and buttress the exercise of power with supernatural sanctions. Machiavelli believed that Christianity by its very nature was an unsatisfactory civil religion, and in the best of all possible worlds he would have liked to see a return to the paganism of ancient Rome, a truly heroic and unified civil religion. But as a practical man he had, with reluctance, to suggest ways in which Christianity might be converted into an almost tolerable religious legitimation of the exercise of power.

Scruton and Machiavelli between them show how acute are the dangers of establishment, in the broadest sense, for the Christian integrity of the church. If Christianity becomes little more than a ceremonial celebration of power and legitimation of the *status quo*, it is lost. For a weak and declining church the attempt to cling on to old patterns of establishment represents a trap and a temptation. But a church which knows that it is not legitimate for it to evacuate the public realm and is aware of the dangers and seductions as well as the opportunities that lie there, still has prudently to organize its relation with the state. Unless it is willing to fulfil some at least of the functions of a civil religion and work within an established and recognized relationship with the state, the church is scarcely able to 'speak truth to power', and is in danger of abdicating one of its God-given responsibilities. A shrewd and moderate position on these issues has been developed by John Habgood, the Archbishop of York, in his book, *Church and Nation in a Secular Age*.[10] He is quite happy to affirm that the church has a function to sustain and reinforce the 'invisible struts and beams' which maintain social cohesion and national unity. This is certainly not the primary task of the church, but it is an important responsibility and opportunity, not unconnected with the gospel, which should not be neglected. The establishment he defends is the present form of the establishment of the Church of England. This is integral to the Church of England's identity as a church rather than a sect or denomination; it serves as a constant reminder, not of privilege but rather of responsibility for all and sundry, for the life of the nation, of the city, of the village, of the parish rather than simply the gathered congregation. The limitations on the freedom of the church which so alarm Tony Benn are trivial in the eyes of the Archbishop of York: 'The formal freedom of the Church of England is not, as I see it, seriously compromised by the fact of establishment. In fact rather the reverse'.[11] Nor is he in any way concerned lest political influence in the making of church appointments might inhibit the voice of prophetic criticism. Political influence here is strictly hedged about and serves as little more than a reminder that a national as well as an ecclesiastical interest ought to be taken into account. But despite all modifications and reforms in recent years, establishment at its heart is a device for bringing into proximity the leaders of the established church and the wielders of political power in a whole range of contexts. This presents dangers and opportunities, admirably summed up by Habgood:

> A church which includes within its activities a ministry towards those with secular power, whether at national or local level, is bound to react differently from one whose 'prophecy' is delivered from a distance. This can look like subservience. 'Power corrupts', says the critic. And if it does not actually corrupt, at least it generates caution, the fear of losing favour and privileges. There is an uncomfortable element of truth in such accusations.
>
> But there is more truth, at least within my own experience, in the perception that the key difference made by proximity to secular power is not one of attitude, but one of knowledge. To be close to those in power is to have some first-hand knowledge of the complexity of the actual choices facing them. This has a devastating effect on prophetic certainties. And actually to share responsibility is even more devastating.[12]

The powerful need help, help of a sort that an established church is in an ideal position to provide: they need to be encouraged to hold fast to a distant, simple vision, and cope with the complex and ambiguous choices which face them day by day. The danger for an established church is that it will so stress the second responsibility that it will lose the knack of pointing steadily to the simple vision. But the balance may be redressed if an established church maintains close ecumenical relations with other, more 'prophetic', churches.

John Habgood is no Roger Scruton, but they both express in very different ways a fundamentally conservative attitude. Scruton significantly prefaces his book with a quotation from 'the judicious Hooker' which might almost, with appropriate stylistic modernizations, have been lifted from Habgood's book. Neither can accommodate or effectively respond to the kind of criticisms preferred by Tony Benn. Habgood presents quite the strongest and most balanced argument for more or less the present form of the establishment of the Church of England which has been presented in recent years. But this system still seems quaint, dangerous and even offensive to multitudes of Christians, especially those who have experienced determined efforts by the political authorities to control and use the church. Habgood's style of establishment may work reasonably satisfactorily when the participants on both sides are moderate, tolerant and conscientious people. But other scenarios are possible, even in Britain. Could the Church of England as at present established resist successfully a persistent attempt, backed by a parliamentary majority, to force her into the mould prepared for an established church by Roger Scruton, to say nothing of E. R. Norman? And even if one sets aside for the moment the possibility that the church might be a prophetic community, surely the sympathy for the complexities of choice faced by decision makers so well expressed by John Habgood as something which has 'a devastating effect on prophetic certainties' must be balanced by a closeness to the poor and the powerless which alone can enable the church to speak for them to the powerful – which is surely close to the essence of what prophecy is.

My colleague Robin Gill has argued that only individuals or small sects can normally be prophetic; churches and denominations are so interwoven with the structure of the society in which they are set that they cannot establish what one might call 'a prophetic distance' enabling them to speak to that society. They may implant Christian values, it is true, but must leave prophecy up to others. Habgood takes the argument one stage further: the church leader cannot be a prophet, apparently because he cannot establish 'prophetic distance' from the power centres of society. Habgood gives qualified assent to Gill's position:

> Churches run great risks . . . if they try as churches to make specific political judgements or take political action. This is not to say that it should never be done. There are times and circumstances when not to do so would be a betrayal, even greater than the betrayal involved in obscuring their distinctive role as witnesses to what lies beyond politics. But the presumption is that in the circumstances of Britain and the British churches today, such occasions are likely to be rare. The involvement, it is constantly said, should be moral rather than political.[13]

And sects, which we are told tend to take absolutist stances and are often eager to 'prophesy', also have difficulties. They are usually encapsulated in ghettoes, cut off from avenues of effective communication with 'the world', isolated groups of 'cognitive deviants' (Berger's phrase) who are not taken seriously by the rest of society.

Yet despite the great risks of which Habgood very properly reminds us, churches as well as individual Christians constantly find themselves forced to move from bland generalities into dealing with the specifics of a situation. There is, in fact, no clearly demarcated frontier between the moral and the political, so that church leaders, synods and assemblies who understand themselves to be proclaiming general principles are commonly, and usually correctly, understood as criticizing policies. Indeed unless a statement of principle has some bearing upon policy it is hard to understand why it should be made. But the important thing is that Christian statements should be seen to be rooted in the gospel rather than derived from some purely political calculus or balancing of interests, or even the promotion of the church as an institution.

Just as there is often a risky but necessary move from the moral to matters of policy, so there is for many people a direct and inevitable route from the pastoral to the political. The most obvious and clear-cut instances are perhaps the notable succession of relatively apolitical pastors who found not long after arrival in South Africa that it was quite impossible to care for people pastorally without being pushed into taking a public political stand, often at great personal cost. Initially this was not infrequently contrary to their understanding of the role of the church and the proper fulfilment of the pastoral office. In the British scene the case of David Sheppard, Bishop of Liverpool, is a case in point. Of impeccable establishment stock and originally espousing a rather individualist and conservative evangelical theology, he responded to pastoral experience first in the inner city in London and then in Liverpool by becoming increasingly radical and outspoken in his account of the social and political implications of the gospel. His book, *Bias to the Poor*,[14] both proclaimed principles and was quite specific in its judgment on policies. It sparked off more controversy than any book by an English bishop since *Honest to God*, and seemed to sound an authentic note of prophecy, as did his later televised Dimbleby Lecture. To be close to the poor and pastorally involved in areas of deprivation and hopelessness seems, in Britain as in Latin America, to generate a new kind of theology which is both pastoral and prophetic. No less significant was the intervention in the coal strike in 1984 first of the Bishop of Durham and then of the Archbishop of Canterbury, representing the majority of the Bishops of the Church of England. In his enthronement sermon Dr Jenkins accepted the role of 'the Bishop who will stand for and serve the whole of the County of Durham, indeed the whole North East', and on that basis called for compromise:

> . . . There must be no victory in the Miners' Strike. There must be no victory, but a speedy settlement which is a compromise pointing to community and the future.
>
> There must be no victory, because the miners must not be defeated. They are desperate for their communities and this desperation forces them to action. . . . But there must be no victory for them on present terms because these include negotiation on their terms alone, pits left open at all costs and the endorsement of civil violence for group ends. Yet, equally, there must be no victory for the Government. This Government, whatever it says, seems in action to be determined to defeat the miners and thus treat workers as not part of 'us'. They also seem to be indifferent to poverty and powerlessness. Their financial measures consistently improve the lot of the already better off while worsening that of the badly off. Their answer to civil unrest seems to be to make the means of suppression more efficient while ignoring or playing down the causes. Such a government cannot promote community or give hope in the very difficult days we are faced with. It cannot even effectively promote the genuine insights it has about the need for realism in what is economically possible. . . . We shall find hope only if more of us are prepared to face up to what is going on, what is wrong in it, and what might be brought out of it.

Neither for the Bishop of Liverpool nor for the Bishop of Durham does the fact that they have close contacts with the powerful in the House of Lords and elsewhere appear to have that 'devastating effect on prophetic certainties' of which the Archbishop of York wrote.[15]

The changes in the relation of church and society in Britain which we discussed earlier in this chapter together with the new ecumenical awareness of the world church bring with them new opportunities and a new freedom. For the church is called to *be* the church, that is, a sign, a promise and an anticipation of the kingdom. And only such a church is capable of filling the 'church-shaped blank' in our society, constantly endeavouring to relate its faith and its theology constructively to long-term issues as well as to immediate policies. And high on its agenda today might be the question of the future of welfare.

7

From Welfare State
to Welfare Society?

I shall not cease from mental fight
Nor shall my sword sleep in my hand
Till we have built Jerusalem
In England's green and pleasant land.
                              William Blake

1. The great debate

Government ministers, most notably Norman Fowler, have repeatedly called in recent days for a 'Great Debate' about the future of the welfare state in Britain. The need for such a fundamental re-examination of the shape and future of welfare in Britain cannot be questioned. As we have seen in earlier sections of this book, everyone is agreed that the welfare state is in need of reform, and some people believe that it needs to be replaced by something radically different. The problems of the welfare state are there for all to see, as are its notable achievements. Hardly anyone desires a continuation of the *status quo*, and economic factors would probably make this impossible in any case. Something must be done – but what?

The specific issues which must be addressed in any thorough-going review of the welfare state are important in themselves, but it should never be forgotten that the underlying question concerns the future shape of British society. How may we most adequately respond to the needs of our neighbours? Is there a better way of tackling the persistent and increasing problem of poverty in Britain, with all the suffering, degradation and exclusion that being poor entails? Is a more just distribution of wealth and income feasible?

77

how may we improve the quality and availability of health care? Is a return to full employment possible, or are there other ways of expressing effectively the worth of each individual and recognizing each person's contribution to the common good? What trade-off is necessary or desirable between the provision of welfare and the production of wealth? Who or what bodies are the most effective providers of welfare – the state, voluntary agencies, the market, the family, and so forth? How can the provision of welfare encourage participation rather than dependence? And all such questions are summed up in the issue of what kind of community, what kind of fellowship, we can have in Britain.

A Great Debate is essential and ought to be a matter of vital concern for Christians. But the way the first stage of the Great Debate for which the Government called has been set up does not inspire great confidence. What was described by the Secretary of State for the Social Services as 'the most substantial examination of the social security system since the Beveridge Report' turned out to be four separate reviews – of pensions, child benefits, housing benefit, supplementary benefit and maternity provision. Whereas Beveridge attempted a co-ordinated and comprehensive overview of British society we are now offered a fragmented series of poorly co-ordinated reviews of specific types of provision. Only part of what one might call the 'Beveridge welfare state' is to be examined; there is no possibility of looking more broadly at the provision of welfare as a whole, or how the various ways of providing welfare affect one another, positively and negatively. Some important kinds of social security provision are excluded from the reviews. Proposals involving increased resources are not to be considered; only changes calling for better use or redeployment of existing human and material resources may be entertained. Unlike Beveridge again, the reviews are firmly under ministerial control, and are to be rushed through at a speed which must make considered judgments difficult, and certainly makes wide participation in this stage of the Great Debate virtually impossible. These hasty, piecemeal and narrowly circumscribed reviews must perforce operate with a very narrow understanding of what welfare is. They are incapable of examining the effects on welfare of fiscal policy, or possibilities of redistribution through taxation. Frank Field's other 'welfare states' which operate to subvert the Beveridge welfare state and channel their benefits predominantly to those already well-off, cannot be scrutinized. It is hard not to suspect that the conclusions have already been determined by the way the reviews were set up, and that these conclusions will fit into a scheme for the gradual dismemberment of the British welfare state and its replacement with something radically different, according to a blueprint already agreed upon before the start of the Great Debate, and basically similar to proposals emanating from the Adam Smith Institute and the Institute of Economic Affairs. The coherence of a whole range of government policies from the abolition of the Royal Commission on the Distribution of Wealth and Income, the encouragement of private medicine and education, the tolerance of an appallingly high level of unemployment, through to taxation and benefit policies which have dramatically increased poverty while making the rich richer suggests that the real unspoken agenda of the Great Debate is demolition rather than reform or reconstruction.

The contrast with Beveridge is striking. He produced a comprehensive and interlocking set of proposals based on ideas which had been germinating for a generation or more in the seed-beds of war and Depression. Beveridge was initially opposed by ministers and senior civil servants; his policies were dismissed as hopelessly utopian and dangerously radical. But they were immediately embraced by the public with immense enthusiasm, thereby starting a real Great Debate in which all sorts of people participated and which in a sense forced the politicians' hands. Even had the Conservatives been returned in 1945 it is likely that they would have been obliged to implement something very like Beveridge's plan, so strong was public feeling and so thoroughly had the major issues been chewed over by the electorate. But war, of course, is a special kind of situation in which hopes are generated and radical restructuring of society seems more possible than it usually does in time of peace. Post-war reconstruction held forth the possibility of implementing ideas about society which had been discussed, tested and examined for decades.

The situation today is very different. Britain is rapidly becoming a post-industrial country in which the question of where the resources for welfare are to be found is bound to become more and more pressing. It is not so much a matter of the looming crisis in welfare expenditure which the 1982 Think Tank found so ominous as the fact that welfare, like other forms of public expenditure, cannot be exempt from the effects of Britain's economic crisis. Poverty, particularly among the elderly and the unemployed, has increased very substantially since 1979, partly as a result of specific government policies. There is widespread disillusion and apathy about possibilities for a better ordering of things. Instead of the kind of alert public which embraced Beveridge's proposals, monitored the behaviour of government and demanded change, we have a mood of deep resignation and fatalism, in many ways more hopeless and ominous than attitudes during the Depression. In a fragmented and callous society the poor and the unemployed and the ethnic minorities are only too often forgotten. When they protest they are labelled 'the enemy within' and treated as a law and order problem. Seldom is it asked why people behave in this kind of way, why they feel alienated from the prosperous part of British society, or what can be done to heal the wounds and engage with protest at its roots.

The government-sponsored Great Debate has understandably aroused a good deal of suspicion, particularly from those who have effectively been excluded from the discussion, and fear that the Great Debate may be little more than a cover for implementing plans derived from bodies such as the Adam Smith Institute and based on the philosophy of possessive individualism. But a more authentic Great Debate is emerging among those who at present have little influence, a debate which today will examine ideas whose time may come tomorrow. In the political wilderness there are opportunities for the nurturing and testing of views and values, policies and projects which will come into their own when the day for reform returns again. 'I am sure', wrote J. M. Keynes, 'that the power of vested interests is vastly exaggerated compared with the gradual encroachment of ideas. Not, indeed immediately, but after a certain interval. . . . But, sooner or later, it is ideas, not vested interests, which are dangerous for good or evil'.[1]

2. Disputed visions

We have seen how R. H. Tawney and many others worked hard and long in the wilderness clarifying values and framing a vision of British society. Tawney in particular contributed vastly to the egalitarian consensus of the 1940s, 50s and 60s, with his emphasis on equality as a condition for fellowship and also for liberty. He communicated his vision, which he recognized as being shaped by Christian faith, in largely secular terms; and he also engaged with the realities of politics, framing policies and proposing a strategy by means of which he hoped his vision might be realized in face of the inevitable opposition of vested interests. Ideas developed in the wilderness gradually encroached until they were commonly taken for granted and deeply influenced the attitudes and policies of the powerful. But now, once again, visions and values are in dispute.

Sir Keith Joseph and Jonathan Sumption's book *Equality* (1979) is a broadside against consensus egalitarianism. They challenge 'one of the central prejudices of modern British politics', that equality is a proper goal of politics and economics. Modern ideas of equality, they assert, cannot be traced back to the New Testament, nor are they rooted in the Christian tradition. Christianity, it appears, teaches that differences of status and of wealth have no significance before God, but this does not impinge on social policy in any way. William Temple and R. H. Tawney are vigorously taken to task for suggesting just this. Against Tawney's belief that a greater equality was necessary for human fellowship, Joseph and Sumption argue that 'brotherhood . . . is necessarily destroyed by the abrasive measures which are required to make men equal'.[2] 'Worthy and thoughtful men' like Temple and Tawney may have an elevated aspiration to equality; they do not realize that 'the reality of equality is grubby and unpleasant'.[3] 'It is not only the route to equality which is unpleasant', they continue, 'but the destination. A society which has achieved a high degree of economic equality would be horrible to live in. It would probably be economically backward and would certainly be culturally stagnant.'[4] The swash-buckling rhetoric is more assertion than argument. Such thread as there is consists of the belief that human nature is fundamentally selfish and acquisitive, and apparently that the flourishing of society depends on the refusal to put restraint on self-interest and avarice, for private vices add up to public benefit. And, besides, there is an underlying conviction that values are no more than fundamental emotional preferences. The egalitarian vision is today in doubt; equality and the other underlying values of the welfare state are in dispute. For Joseph and Sumption the free market supplemented by a modicum of charity can provide as much welfare as is good for society. Besides, the need is not great, for 'by any absolute standard there is very little poverty in Britain today'.[5] Arguments like these subtly transform the atmosphere in discussion, decision and action in ways which can be quite alarming.

Consider, for instance, the case of the Black Report on *Inequalities in Health*. In 1977 David Ennals, at that time Secretary of State for Health and Social Security, set up a Working Group on Inequalities in Health under the chairmanship of Sir Douglas Black, the Chief Scientist at the Department of Health and Social Security. The Working Group was to examine differences in health status between the social classes and the causes of these differences, to compare the situation in Britain with that in other industrial countries, and to explore the implications of their findings for policy. The government of the time was clearly deeply concerned at the obvious serious disparities in health standards and provision, and in the uptake of health care between the different classes. 'The first step towards remedial action', said David Ennals, 'is to put together what is already known about the problem . . . it is a major challenge for the next ten or more years to try to narrow the gap in health standards between different social classes.'[6] The Group found that despite more than thirty years of a National Health Service committed to equal care for all, there remained 'a marked class gradient in standards of health'. Put baldly, the poorer sections of the community tended to die earlier and suffered from a notably higher incidence of sickness, disability and mental illness than the more prosperous groups, and in addition poor people had markedly greater difficulty than richer people in gaining access to medical care, and the quality of the care available to them was often inferior. Those who need the health service most, for a variety of reasons made less use of it. Inequalities in care were found to have been seriously exacerbated since the late 1970s by the considerable increase of the private medical sector. The Group stood foursquare behind the basic principles of the National Health Service – that health care of high quality should be available to everyone on an equal basis, according to need rather than ability to pay. But their enquiries revealed a worsening situation of acute inequalities in health and in medical provision which offended against the fundamental principles underlying the establishment of the National Health Service.

The remedy proposed by the Group was comprehensive and far-reaching. The health and social services should adopt three priorities: first, ensuring that children have a better start in life; secondly, improving the quality of life for disabled people, who commonly bear a heavy burden of cumulative ill-health and deprivation, thereby reducing the need for institutional care; and, thirdly, an emphasis on preventative and educational action to encourage good health. But the Group also affirmed that, while the health and social services should play a major role, serious and offensive inequalities in health would not be removed without a reduction in differences in standard of living. In particular the Group called for a comprehensive anti-poverty strategy, recognizing that poverty, like its frequent associate unemployment, generates much ill-health. In other words, a radically unequal society which tolerates a high level of poverty cannot expect to avoid inequalities in health and in medical care.

The Black Report was received by the new Conservative Government with at least as much embarrassment as had greeted the Beveridge Report from certain circles of the establishment some decades earlier. At first the report was not printed; only 260 duplicated copies were run off, and circulation was accordingly severely limited, even within the National Health Service. Patrick Jenkin, the Secretary of State for Social Services, noted that, 'it will come as a disappointment to many that over long periods since the inception of the NHS there is generally little sign of health inequalities in Britain actually diminishing and, in some cases, they may be increasing'.[7] He then stated firmly that the government could not endorse the Group's proposals, on the ground that they involved too much additional expenditure. But there were certainly other grounds as well for the government's rejection of the report. The argument so convincingly presented by the Working Group that inequalities in health will only be overcome in a more equal society directly conflicts with the view we encountered in Joseph and Sumption's book – that equality is an *un*desirable thing, and that a high level of economic, and by implication also health, inequality is good for society. To the new anti-egalitarians there is nothing wrong as such with unequal provision. But the report's meticulously documented demonstration of what inequality in health means, and how it affects people and society, was a direct challenge to the new vision of an economically dynamic, competitive and radically unequal society, unconcerned about issues of social justice and fair distribution of health care or anything else. Two conflicting visions met in head-on collision. The Black Report was a product of the very best strand in the old consensual vision; Patrick Jenkin was the spokesman for a revived Victorian vision of society, which is explicitly and emphatically against equality. The positive side of this vision is by no means so clear, save that it is highly individualistic, believes in the beneficence of the omnipotent free market, and understands most relations between people as commercial transactions.

It is not easy to handle such conflicts between comprehensive but opposed visions of society. The government reacted to the Black Report with embarrassment and tried to suppress it. No effort was made to meet its arguments or propose an alternative way of responding to the problem, perhaps because it was not recognized as being a problem at all. Patrick Jenkin simply used the disturbing evidence contained in the report to suggest that the NHS had been singularly unsuccessful in achieving some of its principal stated objectives, but he blandly declined to endorse these goals, or to suggest better ways of reaching them. A different vision implies different goals. There is surely a case for a much more candid and clarifying exploration of alternative visions and competing goals than took place in relation to the Black Report. What we encountered in Joseph and Sumption's book was typical: they made it very clear that they were against equality, but it was not at all precisely spelled out what they were in favour of. How much inequality do they regard as desirable? If the systematic and extreme inequality of apartheid South Africa or Nazi Germany leads to national economic prosperity does it therefore become morally acceptable?

The first step in handling any conflict of visions and of goals is surely to clarify, positively and negatively, what the visions are, and what the goals may be, and then identify the points of conflict. Clarification is certainly important – without it there is no real way of knowing whether there is a disagreement, and if so what the argument is about. But the next stage is more problematic. Many people believe that the choice of visions, of ultimate goals, of values is purely arbitrary and emotional; conflicts are irresolvable because we are dealing with irrational choices, and arguments between people who hold conflicting values can be no more than the shouting of slogans. But others hold that reasoning about values and visions, although hard, is feasible. There are those who argue that there is a moral predisposition towards equality of treatment because morality must be universalizable: I should treat everyone else as I wish to be treated myself. Hence inequalities need to be justified, but equality requires no justification. John Rawls's *A Theory of Justice* (1972) gives a lengthy and magisterial argument that equality is a central component of the notion of justice, based on a myth of the 'original position'. The myth is to the effect that a group of rational people are set to devise the principles of a society in which they would have no idea of the role they would each play or the status they would occupy. In the original position there is therefore equality, and the principles which are devised will, Rawls argues, seek to perpetuate equality because no one in the original position would willingly or rationally envisage a situation as being fair in which he or she was disadvantaged. Justice is fairness, and social goods should be equally distributed unless an unequal distribution can be justified as being to the advantage of the least favoured, or significantly for the good of the whole community. It is not necessary to follow Rawls through his six hundred pages of careful

84

argument to realize that something strange has been going on: the human equality which emerges as the conclusion was quietly fed into the account of the original position as something so obvious as to require no defence or explanation. But is this not a presupposition so deeply embedded in cultures related to the Judaeo-Christian tradition that it seems axiomatic, a fundamental fact about human nature, whereas in other contexts – say traditional Hindu India – there was no less deeply entrenched a presumption of human inequality?

The most sustained challenge to Rawls's view is Robert Nozick's *Anarchy, State and Utopia* (1974). Once again the argument purports to be severely rational, but on closer inspection value presuppositions are smuggled in without adequate explanation or defence. It is therefore not surprising that philosophers and social theorists of the eminence of Alasdair MacIntyre and F. von Hayek should now despair of a purely rational grounding and defence of values and of visions of society, and (rather than returning to the old superficial view that they are arbitrary, irrational and ultimately incapable of elucidation) should search for the religious roots of visions and values, through which people strive to make sense of their world. For Christians, this means a new challenge to explore and commend the social vision which arises out of Christian faith, working on the Christian ground and shaping of social values. And this cannot be done without engaging in dialogue and controversy with alternative visions and systems of social values.

This responsibility is made all the more urgent by the inadequacy and fragility of the theory of the welfare state. We have suggested that value and religious presuppositions undergird even the most apparently rational of social theories. Such theory of the welfare state as exists certainly rests on value premises, and from Tawney onwards this has been recognized, although not always with Tawney's awareness of the relationship of values and religion. But these values were rarely subjected to critical examination – during the consensus years the values of the welfare state were very much taken for granted, there was discussion within narrowly circumscribed limits, and those who deviated from consensus values were simply excluded from the debate. Hence there emerged a rather piecemeal theory of the welfare state which was largely pragmatic and recognized the importance of values, but seldom the significance of religion. It sought a society based on and encouraging a high degree of altruism, as commended in Richard Titmuss' comparison of the British blood donation scheme with the American free market in blood, *The Gift Relationship* (1970). This rather loose understanding of theory went with a deep devotion to 'the facts', and was accordingly not uncongenial to the Anglo-Saxon tradition. But it took a great deal for granted, and was only really viable as long as a fundamental consensus on values persisted, as long, that is, as there was a shared vision in Britain. By 1976 a senior statesman of social welfare, William A. Robson, declared, 'There is at present no philosophy of the welfare state and there is an urgent and deep need for such a theory'.[8] For the welfare state was now being confronted with an aggressive and coherent ideology of the New Right, hard-headed and bent on destruction, to which it finds it difficult to respond effectively.

In such a situation Christians should not expect to be able to produce a 'Christian theory of the Welfare state' – Christianity just does not operate like that. But they can and must do some hard work on the Christian grounding of social values, and commend, after re-examination and perhaps amendment in the light of experience, a Christian vision. The task that Richard Tawney fulfilled so superbly in his day requires to be done afresh in ours. One of Tawney's leading disciples, Richard Titmuss recognized the central significance of values:

> We all have our values and prejudices . . . we have a responsibi-
> lity for making our values clear, and we have a special duty to do
> so when we are discussing such a subject as social policy which,
> quite clearly, has no meaning at all if it is considered to be neutral
> in terms of values.[9]

In a period of fundamental consensus about values, when social policy is primarily about adjustments and improvements within an agreed framework, it may be enough to be honest and direct in explaining one's value commitments. But in a more contentious era more is required – it is necessary to explore the roots of one's values and to defend one's values, for they are no longer accepted as self-evident. Another of Tawney's disciples, Peter Townsend, freely recognizes that his fundamental attitudes to people and to society are those customarily regarded as Christian but now widely held by people of no specific religious commitment.[10] But there is a problem here, increasingly widely recognized: residual Christian values now separated from their religious roots and unsupported by Christian belief may in the long run prove difficult to sustain. Some see a tragedy unfolding as basic social values and visions of a better social order are emptied of their spiritual content and transformed in consequence into something almost banal. In a fascinating essay in the volume *Conviction*, Iris Murdoch saw the decline of religion as posing a major crisis for social theory:

> There is a serious and growing void in our thinking about moral and social problems. This void is uneasily felt by society at large and is the more distressing since we are now perhaps for the first time in our history feeling the loss of religion as a consolation and guide. . . . A religious and moral vocabulary is the possession of a few; and most people lack the words with which to say just what is felt to be wrong. . . . Now, for a larger vision, we have to look back to Laski or Tawney, or search for hints in eccentric and little known works by Christians or Marxists.[11]

The most important change since these words were written has been the renaissance of broad-gauge social theory especially among Marxists and the New Right. But the void created by the loss of a religious vocabulary persists, and is increasingly recognized as a major problem both by those who used to put their trust in a value-free or pragmatic social science, and by those who hoped that a purely rational basis for social theory could be found. All this suggests powerfully that a continuing responsibility is laid upon the church, even as it is struggling to come to terms with its new status as a minority in a pluralistic society, to persevere with urgency in the exploration, sustaining and commending of a Christian social vision, and on this basis to contribute to the debate about the goals for society.

3. From vision to policy

Christian social concern is not limited to the inculcation of values and the sustaining of visions; there is also a responsibility for the critical handling of matters of application and implementation, for policy, in short. We have discussed William Temple as an instance of this concern for the movement from vision to policy. Temple held that in the areas of politics and economics 'the main task of the Church must be to inculcate Christian principles and the power of the Christian spirit'.[12] There is, he believed, no such thing as a Christian blue-print for the perfect social order which could be used as the programme for a Christian political party. Nor are there policies which are unambiguously Christian, because matters of application are always involved in ambiguity and compromise. But the church must stand for an 'ordered system of principles' derived from fundamental Christian belief, and providing general guidance, an orientation, relevant to every decision which has to be made and every choice between policy options. The generality of the principles or values which are inculcated needs to be stressed. It is a predisposition towards justice, or equality, or freedom which is implanted rather than specific norms which are immediately applicable. Matters of application were seen as complex and controversial and had to be left to individual Christians to work out in the light of the general guidelines and whatever relevant expertise might be available. General principles act like the hiker's compass: they tell him the direction he should go, but tell him nothing about where to cross this river, or how to negotiate that bog. To deal with *these* problems the walker needs more than the compass – he must consult his map, have a careful look at the terrain, and rely on his companions, and his own experience, on lessons learned in the past. But the compass remains vital, especially when the weather deteriorates and decisions become more difficult and entail greater risks. Without it one may go in the wrong direction or wander around in circles. But even with a compass and a map and in perfect weather conditions we seldom travel in a straight line – we have to find a way around obstacles, we take account of contours, we turn aside to find a camp-site or forage for food.

Temple was both deeply concerned about the application of the Christian vision in social policy and aware that varying and sometimes contradictory policies might be derived from a shared vision. He realized that there were limits to the theologian's competence – he has no special expertise enabling him to act as a kind of theologian-king in the political realm. Visions cannot easily be translated into the terms of the politics of compromise, adjustment and trade-offs. To suggest that Christianity is nothing but a political programme is to diminish, if not deny, the gospel. Accordingly Temple gathered around himself a remarkable circle of theologians, social scientists, philosophers, politicians and civil servants who, over a period of several decades, gave immense energy to investigating the social and political bearing of the Christian gospel. These years of hard work lay behind the Christian contribution to the making of the welfare state in Britain, and without this sustained and serious engagement with the problems in the 1920s and 30s the Christian voice in the 1940s would have been thin and lacking in authority.

The method used in this work, the so-called 'middle axiom' method, is based on a profound conviction that Christianity is relevant to issues of policy. It has a proper awareness of the importance and of the limits of theology. Theologians on their own cannot negotiate this terrain; their contribution is indispensable, but they must themselves listen attentively to social scientists and to practitioners. The method is necessarily inter-disciplinary; the contributions of the various participants are complementary. The facts are to be treated with respect – without close attention to the facts of the case the Christian easily takes flight into irrelevant moralism. And there must be an awareness of the constraints under which the practitioners work. Middle axioms are a form of mediation, a kind of filter paper if you like, between the truths of Christian faith and the detailed and complex decisions with which politicians and administrators are faced. There are four stages in middle axiom thinking. The foundation is the Christian faith, understood in a fairly general way, and a few decades ago far more widely accepted within Western societies than it is today. From this foundation come fundamental ethical principles which are integral to Christian faith, even if most of them are shared by many who do not profess that faith. These are among the values which William Temple believed it was the church's task to inculcate and nurture. As he put it:

> Freedom, Fellowship, Service – these are the three principles of Christian social order, derived from the still more fundamental Christian postulates that Man is a child of God and is destined for a life of eternal fellowship with Him.[13]

Middle axioms mediate between general statements of Christian principle and concrete decisions. They are derived, according to R. H. Preston, by bringing alongside one another Christian theology and Christian principles on the one hand and a detailed understanding of the complexities of the situation under consideration on the other.[14] The two interact, in a way that is nowhere adequately analysed, to produce middle axioms. 'It is these', wrote J. H. Oldham, 'that give relevance and point to the Christian ethic. They are an attempt to define the directions in which, in a particular state of society Christian faith must express itself. They are not binding for all time, but are provisional definitions of the type of behaviour required of Christians at a given period in given circumstances'.[15] One might speak of middle axioms as middle range social goals. After the war the kind of middle axioms which were being promulgated involved opposition to racism, the need for an international organization to help maintain peace and encourage co-operation among nations, and the responsibility of government to strive to maintain full employment. William Temple, in the sixth chapter of *Christianity and Social Order*, outlines a series of middle axioms relating to family life, the sanctity of the individual, education, fellowship, and economic justice. But application is a more contentious matter, and certainly one in which an archbishop has no particular authority. Temple puts his own ideas as to implementation into an appendix, well aware that many who share his faith, his principles and his middle axioms will differ from him about how these should be applied.

Middle axiom thinking has been immensely influential and productive in Christian social ethics since the 1930s. But there are problems which have made it notably less attractive in recent times. The first difficulty relates to application. As we have seen, middle axiom thinkers admit that contrary and diverse applications can arise from an agreed middle axiom and are strongly resistant to saying that any one decision or course of action flows necessarily from a middle axiom and can therefore be called Christian. Middle axiom thinking still operates at a far higher level of generality than many of its proponents wish to suggest, and offers remarkably little specific guidance either of a positive nature or by way of exclusion. Uneasiness in face of conflict and division is also characteristic. It operates most effectively when there is a broad respect for Christian standards, a general agreement about the nature of Christian values, and few fundamental conflicts about long-term goals. In short, middle axiom thinking works best in a society which recognizes itself as being in some general sense Christian, in which there is a high degree of consensus, and in which the social order is held not to be in need of radical recasting. In a more pluralistic situation, where there are fundamental conflicts about values, or in a time of crisis, middle axiom procedures seem less appropriate and productive. 'In face of Auschwitz' the issues are so clear-cut that the movement from Christian faith to a particular political option appears less complex and a confessional rather than a cautious middle axiom approach is called for. In the German Church Struggle, for example, the Christians who subscribed the Barmen Declaration (1934) were proclaiming that their differences with those who were willing to co-operate or compromise with the Nazis were a fundamental and irreconcilable theological conflict, with unavoidable ethical and political consequences. In such a situation there is not, and must not be, the degree of consensus that middle axiom thinking requires for its operation. But in less extreme and more confusing contexts

Christians rightly fall back on something like middle axiom procedures.

In the second place, middle axiom thinking is elitist, as I have argued elsewhere.[16] Theologians and church leaders produce the model of Christianity and the statement of general Christian principles; in discussion with social scientists and other 'experts' they develop middle axioms; and finally application is handed over to the individual Christian citizen, on the assumption that many of them are in positions of leadership and influence. What is lacking here is the view from the bottom of the social heap, the opinions of the poor and the deprived, the feelings of 'those whose feet the shoe pinches'. And this lack is of quite crucial importance. Between them the doctrine of sin and the sociology of knowledge should serve to remind us that social position, even in theology, influences the way one thinks, and theologians, church leaders, experts, and politicians are, on the whole, of fairly high social status. Latin American experience over the last few decades should teach us how theology and the church can be revitalized by attending to the view from the bottom of the heap, and making the poor *participants* in theological and ethical thinking. Theology is too important to be left to the theologians.

In the third place, the sharp differentiation between principle and application indicates an awkward distinction between theory and practice. The church generates principles and middle axioms out of a static, consensual and abstract understanding of the Christian faith. Action then becomes the implementation of a theory arrived at independently by different people. Practice must conform to theory, but is in no sense a source of theory, except that the 'practical man' may introduce some caveats into the process at the middle axiom stage. It is neat, but its very neatness can disguise the facts that theology, ethics and action interact at every stage, so that it is far too simple to speak of deriving policies from a static, given and propositional deposit of faith, or that the church as such can opt out of policy disputes any more than it can disregard theological conflicts.

There is much in the middle axiom approach which one would wish to see continued: reverence for the facts, modesty about the capacity of theology to 'solve' complex social problems on its own, the need for groups of informed people to grapple over a period of time and with real seriousness with issues before any sort of pronouncement is made, the suggestion that there are usually several options open to the decision-maker which are compatible with the vision, and so on. But an updated method in social theology would need to give attention to ways of articulating the voice from the foot of the pile and encouraging people to share more fully in determining their own future. There needs to be a new balance between seeing the theologian or the church leader as a chaplain to the powerful, to the decision-makers, and his call to be in solidarity with the poor and the marginalized. If the church has a preferential option for the poor, social theology should not be afraid to 'speak for the dumb', listening attentively to the poor, the marginalized and the excluded, and acting as a mouthpiece for them.

4. The conversion of opinion

We examined the Baillie Commission in Scotland as an instance of a major denomination endorsing the broad outlines of the welfare state and mobilizing Christian opinion in its support, encouraging Christians to relate their faith to their political opinions, preferences, options and votes. It is, of course, one of the perennial responsibilities of the church to help believers to shape their attitudes in a Christian way. This also involves attempts to influence and challenge public opinion in society at large. We have seen how there has been a swing of opinion in Britain away from support for the welfare state and towards very negative attitudes to the poor and the unemployed. We noted also that there were indications that attitudes within the churches were significantly harder than in the country at large.

What people believe undoubtedly affects their values, their attitudes, and their behaviour – and hence, how society operates. And changes of belief and of attitude are socially important. Tawney called for what he labelled 'intellectual conversion' to underpin a juster and more fraternal ordering of industrial society.[17] Julian Le Grand concludes his careful demonstration that the 'strategy of equality' has not led to a more equal distribution of resources with an appeal for attitudinal change:

> Ideology is a much more important determinant of social processes than is often supposed. To understand what people believe is crucial to understand the way they behave; and to change the way they behave, it is crucial to change what they believe. Indeed ideology can often override self-interest. . . . A change in beliefs can even induce people to reduce their power and privilege.[18]

Is it, perhaps, too cynical to suggest that this kind of change of attitude, while important, is not in itself enough to fulfil such grandiose expectations? Conversion in itself does not bring in the new Jerusalem; nor does it destroy sin and selfishness. Luther was right to see believers in this world as *simul justus et peccator*, both justified and sinner at the same time. But even if attitudinal change is not a *deus ex machina*, capable of unravelling the complex tangles of the plot in the last few minutes of the play, it is important, and Christians are properly and centrally concerned with it. The process called in Latin America 'conscientization' is based on the belief that people cannot know God truly or play a constructive role in society until they are able to see and understand the realities of the world around them. And – here Marxism has helped in the recovery of Christian insights – it is in changing the world that we find the truth about God, the world and ourselves.

The churches have first to set their own houses in order. Starting from the realization that there are many within the churches who have racist attitudes, who dismiss most of the poor in Britain as feckless scroungers who have brought their fate deservedly upon themselves, and who have highly negative attitudes towards the welfare state and the social services – a serious endeavour must be made to help such people to see that their attitudes are incompatible with the gospel. There should be no surprise that such attitudes exist within the church. They are yet another illustration of the influence of the attractive paganism of capitalist society, where everything is measured in terms of money and 'success' is the only index of worth. A statement like Rhodes Boyson's appeals to many Christians because it is couched in terms of 'moral fibre' and individual responsibility; they do not notice that it is a panygyric on private selfishness and private success at the expense of the 'failures and the feckless':

> The moral fibre of our people has been weakened. A state which does for its citizens what they can do for themselves is an evil state; and a state which removes all choice and responsibility from its people and makes them like broiler hens will create the irresponsible society no-one cares no-one bothers – why should they when the state spends all its energies taking money from the energetic, successful and thrifty to give to the idle, the failures and the feckless?[19]

But ultimately the only way of countering such seductive alternative views and essentially unchristian values is to present and commend the Christian vision of *shalom*, of a community where people care for one another and affirm each other's worth, of a fellowship which is not basically a market or an arena, of the new Jerusalem which is to come, and hope for which is the only aspiration capable of overcoming and displacing the materialistic 'official optimism' of our modern society.

5. *Towards a welfare society*

Those who sought to make a welfare society produced a welfare state, a highly centralized and bureaucratic system, in which the state was seen as the principal, if not ideally the only, provider of welfare. Some of the reasons for this are quite clear. In war-time an unduly rosy view of the state as the altruistic custodian of the common good capable of providing almost anything emerged and lodged in the popular consciousness. Although other providers of welfare were at least formally recognized, they were often tolerated rather than encouraged, for the state saw itself as the provider rather than the enabler of welfare. For very good reasons people were disenchanted with the nightwatchman state or the state which saw its role as that of a referee between competing interests and nothing more. The Big Brother state of Orwell's nightmare was also eschewed – again for very good reasons. But the assumption that the state was an omnipotent provider of all good things, and the solver of all problems led inevitably to a disillusioned reaction. Extreme people spoke of the 'nanny state' which reduces citizens to irresponsible infantile dependence. Irving Kristol, the American New Right theorist, spoke of the welfare state having become 'the paternalistic state, addressing itself to every variety of "problem" and committed to "solving" them all – committed, that is, to making human life unproblematic'.[20] In Britain Professor Anthony King announced that the state was trying 'to play God', and must be stopped. Moderate and caring people began to realize that the social security office or the doctor's waiting room did not very markedly and obviously encourage fraternity, and that the bureaucracy had its own interests, which made it hard for it not to strive for a monopoly of caring rather than building up a participative welfare society.

Christians have been perennially suspicious of states which usurp the place of God and claim 'to make human life unproblematic'. They refused in the early days to take part in the civil cult of the Roman Empire or burn incense to Caesar, affirming the while in the strongest possible terms that the state had a mandate, a responsiblity from God and played a role in the fulfilment of his purposes. The dominant image of political authority in the Old Testament, which is important in the New as well, is that of the shepherd king, who cares for his people as a shepherd cares for his sheep. There is no ground therefore for denying that the state has a welfare role, but there is no ground either for giving the state a *monopoly* of welfare responsibilities.

In a welfare society of the future a new balance will need to be struck between what the state provides, acting on behalf of the whole community, what is provided by voluntary agencies and local community groups, by the family and so forth. Ways of encouraging a greater sense of participation and giving a greater role to what Peter Berger called 'mediating structures' will have to be found. But the decisions will not be easy ones, and the balance will be delicate, as Richard Titmuss points out:

> In the ultimate analysis society may have to choose between 'the sense of community' on the one hand, with which is equated small-scale and often ineffectively preventive, poor quality services, and larger social groupings offering better quality services, and more freedom of choice for consumers, with the recognized dangers of larger bureaucracies and professional power units. In facing this dilemma the question must be asked whether the purpose is to serve people – and many of the clients are defenceless people – or to advance the interests of established organizations or professional groups.[21]

The pendulum has swung away from an extraordinary faith in the capacity of the state to an even more extraordinary belief in the beneficence of the market. Through the mysterious workings of an invisible hand the market serves the common good and is the most efficient mechanism of distribution, of welfare as of everything else. It is generally accepted by the advocates of the omnipotent market that it encourages inequality and that it is absurd to expect it to operate justly. It is also frequently suggested that the market's effectiveness is always impeded by interference or attempts at regulation. This faith in the paradoxical benevolence of the market needs to be questioned. Of course the market has a place, and a significant place, in almost any economy – even the Chinese now recognize this. But that almost all social relationships should be understood in market terms, that the market should become the dominant *social* institution – that would be quite intolerable. Classical economics argued that the acquisitiveness and selfishness of the market would operate effectively only in a society where it was taken for granted that unselfishness was a good thing. Adam

Smith, for instance, saw economic activity as the one sphere of human life where self-interest should be dominant; elsewhere the 'moral sentiments' of sympathy, disinterested concern for one's fellows, and so forth, must hold undisputed sway; only thus could the effects of economic self-interestedness be made acceptable. More recent attempts to extend the market to encompass more and more of life have allowed the 'market ethic', which by itself is socially destructive, to undercut and erode the countervailing values upon whose strength in the past the proper working of the market depended. Suggestions that the omnipotent market is the only institution capable of solving the problem of poverty or the necessary counterpart to participative democracy must be viewed with suspicion – there is too much evidence to the contrary. And that the *unregulated* market is the most efficient, the most natural, and the fairest mechanism for the distribution of welfare seems absurd – but that is not to say that the market has *no* place in welfare provision.

6. The Jerusalem that is to come

It has been aptly remarked that most of the argument about the future shape of British society has been between those who wish to return to the 'golden age' of the 1920s or perhaps the Victorian era, and those who wish to recapture the first, fine, careless rapture of the inauguration of the welfare state in the 1940s. Any Christian contribution should be dominated by a hope that is communal, and indeed political – the hope for the kingdom, for the New Jerusalem, for the city whose builder and maker is God. The myth of origin may be of Adam, but from the beginning he is in fellowship with God, and human company is soon provided, for 'it is not good for man to be alone'. All the images of the goal are communal, and indeed political: Christianity is not about the 'flight of the Alone to the Alone', but about the search for fellowship in its fullness, for a social order that is harmoniously structured. The Christian faith is about *shalom*, about the kingdom, about *koinonia* (communion or fellowship); it therefore necessarily looks towards the flourishing of people in society. Love towards God and love towards neighbour are inextricably linked together in the Great Commandment in such a way that the Christian should have no time for atomic individualism. When Enoch Powell says, 'Man . . . is born as an individual, he dies as an individual, and if there is forgiveness and redemption, he is forgiven and redeemed as an individual. It is to man the individual that the Gospel speaks',[22] he is uttering a dangerous half-truth, by denying that the Christian hope is a collective hope. This kind of individualism is attractive to many in our day, not because it has been there in the tradition from the beginning – which it has not – but because it tunes it so harmoniously with the popular, but pagan, philosophy of possessive individualism and relegates the Christian faith to the private and personal realm where it is less of a disturbance. Possessive individualism understands welfare largely in terms of individuals and families seeking to improve their condition, develop their capacities, and pursue their interests with the minimum of state regulation and little explicit regard for other people. F. von Hayek can even say, 'The general obligation to help and sustain one another, . . . for the lack of which the Great Society is generally blamed, is incompatible with it'.[23] The love-command and the injunction to seek first the kingdom and its justice are no longer applicable in the Great Society, the modern industrial state; people are set free even from the traditional call for altruism and benevolence, it would seem. And this extraordinary position is legitimated by the mystical and unsubstantiated belief that individuals' uninhibited pursuit of their own interests will cumulatively promote the common good. This position has its attractions for two groups of Christians in particular: for old-fashioned Lutherans who draw an extraordinarily sharp division between the two Kingdoms and proclaim the secular world to be radically autonomous, following its own principles which are only eschatologically related to the gospel; and conservative evangelicals and pietists who have absorbed Enlightenment individualism and allowed it to dominate even their understanding of the faith. But most Christians properly understand the tradition as affirming that human flourishing and human welfare are only possible in community, that it is only in fellowship that women and men find fulfilment. The gospel is the good news of the kingdom, not a word in the ear of the individual concerning his private morals and personal destiny.

The kingdom is a gift, already received in promise and in part, to the full realization of which we look forward and for which we pray. And it is also a call, to engage in the work of the kingdom, to act as a citizen of the kingdom now, to anticipate its full arrival. Hence we pray, 'Thy kingdom come, thy will be done on earth as it is in heaven'. And praying for the coming of the kingdom is inseparable from working for the kingdom; otherwise the prayer is hypocritical. And to pray that God's will be done on earth is to identify ourselves, the church, and the world with its states, nations and societies, as the sphere in which God's will is to be done *now* in which we are to look for, and work for, anticipatory realizations of the kingdom.

But the kingdom and the other great eschatological images of community as God wills it to be are not blueprints that can be implemented here and now, in such a broken, sinful world as this. There is a necessary gap between vision and policy; but that does not mean that they should not be related. For policy without vision is directionless and vapid, and a vision which has no policy implications is a pipe-dream. Hence a major function of the church is to point insistently to the vision, while exploring and sustaining it. A proper awareness of the provisionality, limits and partiality of all earthly realizations of the kingdom should not depress. The kingdom is a sign of hope, and a sign which contrasts sharply with the frothy official optimism of our modern societies. It calls us to press forward; learning from the past while continuing to be obedient to the heavenly vision; a pilgrim people who are not at ease amid the injustices of our present society, or reconciled to things as they are.

Both church and civil society are orientated towards the kingdom; each in its own way should point to the kingdom; in each God's will is to be done; and at the end both will be absorbed into the one great fellowship of *shalom*, welfare, fulfilment. But the church is called in a special way to be a sign, a promise and an anticipatory manifestation of the kingdom, the place where people learn of the nature of the kingdom and see it already present as a kind of working model of the kingdom. The church proclaims the good news of the kingdom, and its own life should confirm the truth of the gospel that is preached. This is why the inner life of the church is important – even apparently mundane things like levels of stipend, deployment of resources, structures of authority and decision-making – as well as the more obviously significant things, like the quality of fellowship and the degree of concern for the needs of the world. There is no doubt that the church finds it very hard to *be* the church, to put its life where its voice is. All Christians, more or less, are against racism, or so we are assured. Hundreds of sermons against racism aroused hardly a ripple of dissent. But when the World Council of Churches set up the Programme to Combat Racism and actually gave money to groups fighting it, the solemn assemblies of the church broke out in bitter rancour. Everyone agrees that Christians should be concerned about poverty; but when David Sheppard wrote his book, *Bias to the Poor* (1983), pointing out that there is an increasing amount of grievous poverty in Britain and that specified government policies had plunged far more people into poverty and demonstrated a strong bias *against* the poor, all hell broke loose: a bishop interfering in matters which are none of his concern! But these things *are* the concern of the church of Jesus Christ because it is called to proclaim and to prefigure the kingdom. And to fail to speak or to act would be a sign of faithlessness, a denial of the good news of the kingdom.

The story of the sheep and the goats in Matthew, chapter 25, has been referred to as the *magna carta* of Christian social involvement, and aptly so. It is the nations, not individuals, who are called to account before the Son of Man in his glory, when he comes with all his angels at the last day. The blessed nations are to inherit the kingdom because they have had a care for the welfare of the needy:

> Come, O blessed of my Father, inherit the kingdom prepared for you from the foundation of the world; for I was hungry and you gave me food, I was thirsty and you gave me drink, I was a stranger and you welcomed me, I was naked and you clothed me, I was sick and you visited me, I was in prison and you came to me.
> (Matt. 25.34–36)

The righteous nations have responded to human need with love and justice, with compassion and kindness, refusing to exclude or marginalize the needy in their communities. They are amazed that the Son of Man identifies with the needy; they have been responding to human need rather than attempting to serve the King, whom perhaps they did not know or recognize until they stand before his throne. Without awareness that they were doing anything other than responding to the needs of their fellows, they have been doing the will of God: 'Truly, I say to you, as you did it to one of the least of these my brethren, you did it to me' (Matt. 25.40). And those who say that the 'brethren' mentioned here refers exclusively to the early Christians, who believed that the nations would be judged by their treatment of them, should be alert to the shocking behaviour of Jesus himself, as told in the gospels. He welcomed to his table the outcast and the despised, the notorious sinners and the prostitutes; he established fellowship by reaching out to the leper and the Samaritan; he healed sick people and fed hungry people; he had compassion on the needy; and died on the cross to inaugurate *shalom*. All this was the manifestation of the kingdom, which Christians in every age are called to proclaim and move towards.

The welfare state estabished in the 1940s was a notable experiment in *shalom*, in moving towards the kingdom. Like all endeavours to realize a noble vision, it has been successful only in part. Christians, along with others, should today be putting their energies into analysing and assessing what went wrong, and what went right in this great experiment. The vision that underlay that experiment has faded; but it was not a will-o-the-wisp or a mirage, but a vision closely related to the hope of the coming kingdom. Today our society lacks a compelling and attractive vision. Christians have a continuing responsibility for maintaining visions which are not detached from the problems of society, but illumine them, and provide motivation for a realistic engagement with the possibilities latent in present problems and present crises. Vision may be renewed by those who believe that the faith is more than a private matter and have the courage to engage with the intellectual bankruptcy of the Left and the callous intellectual vigour of the Right. Only on the basis of such renewed vision for this generation can we seek afresh a more caring and compassionate society. William Blake's call comes also to us: 'Let every Christian, as much as in him lies, engage himself openly and publicly before all the World in some mental pursuit for the Building up of Jerusalem.'

Epilogue:
Where Do We Go From Here?

Today the perennial question how love (*agape*) and fellowship (*koinonia*) may be transposed into political and economic terms lies at the heart of the debate about the future of welfare. And it is necessary once more to witness to the fundamental truth that the economy is made to serve people, and people are not made to serve the economy. As we have argued earlier, we should learn from the experience of the welfare state how to refurbish the vision of welfare, and how to build on that experience and develop a more adequate form of what should be called a welfare society. Although the British experience of the welfare state is crucial, we must not allow it to circumscribe our view or narrow the range of possibilities which the realistic visionary may consider. There are other patterns of welfare state, and other ways of providing welfare and building a caring community, which have been tried elsewhere. From some of them we may have much to learn. Austria, for instance, has an outstanding record for full employment with economic growth and industrial peace, combined with a highly developed welfare system, all based on a strong and continuing national consensus and a sense of social partnership. And Sweden's welfare state seems far better equipped than Britain's to weather economic adversity while maintaining – indeed *by* maintaining – a high level of welfare expenditure.[1] It should surprise and shame people in Britain, who once boasted of their welfare state, to realize that now Britain spends less per head of the population on social security and other forms of welfare provision than any other country in the EEC.[2] Indeed, in most other countries of Western Europe welfare expenditure is seen as contributing towards economic prosperity

101

and growth rather than, as in Britain, putting a strain on the economy and attracting the most rigorous cuts in public expenditure.

There are, then, a variety of ways forward for those who are concerned for the future of welfare and the reform of the welfare state. Hard times do not force us to give up a comprehensive provision of welfare as a luxury we can no longer afford, but make the question of a just distribution of welfare more urgent than ever. Evidence from various contexts does not suggest that welfare as such is parasitic on prosperity, or economically destructive. And lessons can be learned from the experience of other countries which suggest that there are a number of ways forward which are realistic political options even in a time of recession, provided the will is there. We should be planning in the light of experience, experiment and basic values, the next steps towards a welfare society in which a strong sense of community rests upon commitment to the welfare of each, and particularly of the weakest and most vulnerable. Richard Titmuss' dream, expressed most fully in his *The Gift Relationship* (1970), that the welfare state would enable the development of a society in which altruistic (or 'gift') relationships would flourish and hence a welfare society would gradually emerge, has only been realized in small part. But the dream remains valid, particularly, perhaps, for the Christian. What are needed are new ways of working towards it.

In a welfare state, as in a welfare society, there are and must be numerous providers of welfare. Many of the most telling criticisms of the welfare state have to do with the balance and relationship between the various providers: in a welfare society there will certainly continue to be a plurality of provision, but the emphases are likely to be different. It is, for instance, important to remember that the family probably continues to be the major provider of welfare within the welfare state, and that this is a highly desirable thing. A mentally handicapped child or a disabled adult is in most circumstances best provided for at home rather than in an institution. And it is good if disabled people are encouraged to operate as normally as possible within the community. But this of course puts great pressures on the immediate carers, and they need support of various kinds from the broader community if they are to be able to continue their caring function effectively and without impossible strain. Hence statutory and voluntary agencies provide a whole range of relief and back-up services, from special equipment and home helps through to tax allowances and improved access for wheelchairs in public transport and public places. But there are situations with which the family cannot cope, and here the broader community has a responsibility to step in and offer institutional care, for example. And since a family's capacity to provide for the welfare of its members varies among other things in relation to the family's resources, support for the family as a major provider of welfare leads directly to the need for some degree of redistribution. To take an extreme case, there is something profoundly offensive in some families having the resources to pamper pet dogs while other families are unable to provide the basic necessities for their children.

Most local communities also have complex and important networks through which welfare is provided. Some of these links are formal, structured and recognized, but most are informal ties of responsibility, care and affection. The person in a tower block or tenement stair who takes a mug of soup each day to a housebound neighbour and checks that he is all right is providing welfare, and should find encouragement and support in doing so. These are the kinds of actions that sustain community, and will always remain the front line of welfare provision, the veins and arteries of a welfare society. Then there is the immense diversity of voluntary agencies. Some may be quaintly old-fashioned or forbiddingly paternalistic and judgmental, but most provide ways in which a community may care for aspects of its own welfare. Voluntary agencies have a good deal of scope for innovation and experiment. They may take risks, support informal and non-professional modes of caring, and encourage a sense of participation in welfare. They are properly seen as complementary to the statutory agencies rather than in competition with them. They certainly should not be regarded as simply a more economical alternative way of providing welfare. Their greatest single advantage is that they stimulate and enable extensive participation in welfare provision and contribute to the mosaic of many forms of caring. They have some funds of their own and can raise finance, but if they are to be recognized as they ought to be as part of the total commitment of the community to welfare they must continue to attract substantial government grants.

The statutory side of welfare provision is divided between the local and the central sectors. Local authorities at various levels have a knowledge of conditions which may allow them to tailor welfare provision to the needs of the area, and they are answerable to a local electorate. Each region has its special problems, its local traditions, and its peculiar facilities. There is a strong case that a diversity in welfare provision between parts of the country should be tolerated or encouraged. But it is necessary also that there should be some redistribution of resources between regions, for the poorer regions on the whole require the greater expenditure on welfare. And the present tendency to make local authorities little more than agents of central government and its policies should cause concern to all who value diversity and believe that welfare provision should be tailored to the needs and circumstances of each region and accountable to the local community.

A good deal has been said earlier in this book about the role of the state in welfare. But even if it is admitted that the welfare state has aroused exaggerated expectations which it has been unable to fulfil, and has developed a confusingly complex, bureaucratic and central-ized welfare system based on the mistaken belief that the state ought to have a virtual monopoly of welfare provision, it remains true that the state has an indispensable role in welfare. The continuing and unavoidable responsibilities of the state in welfare seem to be four:

1. Enabling and encouraging a variety of networks of care;
2. Setting standards for welfare and monitoring that these standards are met;
3. Ensuring a relatively just and fair division of the available resources according to need;
4. Providing certain services directly, particularly those which benefit markedly from economies of scale.

This is by no means incompatible with the devolution of day-to-day responsibility for administration and implementation. For instance, there continues to be an immensely strong case for a *National* Health Service offering as far as possible an equal standard of care to everyone in the country, but this goes very happily with a structure of councils and boards through which the NHS is accountable also to the local community.

The market has always had a role in the provision of welfare, and recently there have been moves to increase that role significantly on the grounds that the market is a mechanism which minimizes costs and maximizes efficiency, preserving freedom by presenting the consumer with choices and regarding him as sovereign. But the market is not a caring agency and its benefits go predominantly to those who are already prosperous rather than to the needy; it tends to concentrate welfare where the money is rather than where the need is. So although the market will continue to play a role in the provision of welfare, its place must not be exaggerated and there must be a shrewd awareness of the limitations of the market.

In a welfare society there will continue to be a plurality of forms of provision of welfare and a new recognition that no mode of provision should have a monopoly, and that there should be a new balance and a recognized complementarity between the various providers of welfare. The state will always have a role, if not perhaps as dominant a role as it has had. It will monitor the provision of welfare, guarding against major disparities between regions and providing certain major services. But it will make no claim to a monopoly of welfare provision, and many responsibilities will be entrusted to local authorities, voluntary agencies, community action, and the family. The market will continue to have a place, but it will be recognized that it is not a peculiarly appropriate instrument for the allocation of welfare. Hadley and Hatch's proposals for an alternative system of welfare provision suggest a possible way of moving from a welfare state to a welfare society. They sum up their suggestions as

1. Plural provision. A greater proportion of all forms of social service would be provided by voluntary organizations, the one major exception being social security. Thus instead of expanding the statutory services, there would grow up alongside them a variety of community-based initiatives.

2. Decentralisation and community orientation of statutory services. The predominant mode of statutory provision would be the community-oriented one, implying flatter structures, a different interpretation of professionalism and reinforcement as opposed to replacement of informal sources of care.

3. Contractual rather than hierarchical accountability. In return for funding and the contracting out of more services to voluntary organization, government, both local and central, would exercise a stronger monitoring and inspecting role than at present. Thus there would be more emphasis on maintaining accountability through contractual agreements as opposed to the exercise of authority within hierarchies.

4. Participation in representation. The counterpart of greater monitoring and inspection would be the participation of consumers and providers in statutory decision-making. Thus the representatives of users and providers would sit on local authority committees. . . . This would mean a substantial

dilution, or perhaps rather enrichment, of the pure doctrine of representative democracy, legitimacy would cease to reside exclusively with representatives selected by existing methods.[3]

These proposals represent a way of moving towards what the World Council of Churches calls a 'just, participatory and sustainable society'. Such a welfare society would recognize that justice, as the political expression of love, is the basis of true fellowship. It would be concerned about fairness and would show a particular bias towards the poor in policy making and in the allocation of welfare and of resources. It would regard as intolerable the fact that the poor and the unemployed bear so disproportionate a share of the costs of economic recession and would be sceptical of the suggestion that the best incentive for the rich is the carrot and for the poor the stick.[4] Participation involves efforts to lessen social divisions and help people to take on responsibility for their communities by sharing in decision-making. Poverty, economic and social inequality and racism all involve exclusion from community and from significant involvement in the decisions which affect one's destiny. Paternalism and a false professionalism draw a sharp and socially disruptive distinction between the providers and the clients or recipients of welfare. In a welfare society this distinction must be overcome. And the only sustainable form of a welfare society can be one in which economic and social policy are closely co-ordinated, and welfare is not seen as a separate issue but as a central dimension in all policy-making. In particular there must be an integration of taxation and welfare policies. Tax allowances and reliefs involve more money than the entire social security budget, yet in some cases they operate on directly opposed principles.

In a welfare society men and women learn that they are dependent upon one another, that they have gifts to give to one another, and that the welfare of the individual or the group cannot be achieved in isolation from, or at the expense of, others. For we all belong to the one human family, and its welfare in fellowship is something for which Christians are bidden both to work and pray.

Notes

2. The Stirrings of Conscience

1. John Habgood, *Church and Nation in a Secular Age*, Darton, Longman & Todd 1983; Robin Gill, *Prophecy and Praxis*, Marshall, Morgan & Scott 1981.
2. David Donnison, *The Politics of Poverty*, Robertson 1982, p. 132.
3. Henry Fielding, *A Proposal for Making an Effectual Provision for the Poor*, 1753.
4. Peter Golding and Sue Middleton, *Images of Welfare: Press and Public Attitudes to Poverty*, Robertson 1982, p. 43.
5. William H. Beveridge, *The Pillars of Security*, Allen & Unwin 1943, pp. 107–108.
6. Peter Townsend in Norman Mackenzie (ed.), *Conviction*, MacGibbon and Kee 1958, p. 93.
7. Ibid., p. 94.
8. Richard Titmuss, cited in Asa Briggs 'The Welfare State in Historical Perspective', *Archives Europeennes de Sociologie*, Vol. 2, no. 2, pp. 221–58.
9. George Orwell, *The Lion and the Unicorn: Socialism and the English Genius*, Penguin Books 1982, p. 102.
10. Orwell, ibid., p. 74.
11. Ibid., p. 113.
12. *The Times*, 1 July 1940, cited in Derek Fraser, *The Evolution of the British Welfare State*, Macmillan 1973, p. 265.

3. The Building of the Welfare State

1. Arthur Marwick, *British Society Since 1945*, Penguin Books 1982, p. 63.
2. Richard Titmuss, *Essays on 'The Welfare State'*, Allen & Unwin, 3rd edition 1976, p. 4; *Commitment to Welfare*, Allen & Unwin 1968, pp. 124–5.

3. Fraser, *The Evolution of the British Welfare State*, p. 222.
4. Asa Briggs, 'The Welfare State in Historical Perspective', p. 228.
5. David Thomson, *Equality*, Cambridge University Press 1969, p. 220.
6. Churchill cited by Fraser, op. cit., pp. 202–203.
7. *Beveridge Report*, paras 7–9, cited in Susanne MacGregor, *The Politics of Poverty*, Longman 1981, p. 9.
8. J. C. Kincaid, *Poverty and Equality in Britain: A Study of Social Security and Taxation*, Penguin Books, revised edition 1975, pp. 29–31.
9. E.g. C. A. R. Crosland, *The Future of Socialism*, Cape 1956, p. 59.
10. Jose Harris, *William Beveridge*, Clarendon Press 1977, pp. 27–30.
11. Beveridge, *The Pillars of Security*, pp. 33–40.
12. F. A. Hayek, *The Road to Serfdom*, Chicago 1944.
13. R. H. Tawney, *Equality*, Allen & Unwin 1964, p. 222.
14. Kincaid, op. cit., pp. 121–26.
15. David Donnison, *The Politics of Poverty*, p. 21.
16. Anthony Sampson, *The Changing Anatomy of Britain*, Hodder & Stoughton 1982, p. 75.

4. Christian Contributions

1. R. H. Tawney quoted in J. M. Winter and D. M. Joslin, *R. H. Tawney's Commonplace Book*, Cambridge University Press 1972, p. 67.
2. Tawney, *The Acquisitive Society*, Bell & Son 1921, (new edition with Preface by Peter Townsend, Harvester Press 1982) p. 230.
3. Tawney, *Religion and the Rise of Capitalism*, 1926, Penguin Books 1938, p. 280.
4. Winter and Joslin, op. cit., p. 68.
5. Ibid., pp. 53–54.
6. Tawney, *The Acquisitive Society*, p. 227.
7. Tawney, *Equality*, p. 56.
8. Ibid., p. 118.
9. Ibid., p. 105.
10. Ibid., p. 164.
11. Ibid., p. 56.
12. Ibid., p. 145.
13. See R. H. Preston, *Religion and the Persistence of Capitalism*, SCM Press 1979, pp. 89–110.
14. Reinhold Niebuhr, cited in Alan Suggate, 'Reflections on William Temple's Social Ethics', *Crucible*, October–December 1981, pp. 155–63, p. 155.
15. Neil McIlwraith, 'William Temple: A Christian Understanding of the State', unpublished typescript 1982.
16. William Temple, *Christianity and Social Order*, Penguin Books 1942, p. 75.
17. F. A. Iremonger, *William Temple*, Oxford University Press 1948, p. 438.

18. Keith Joseph and J. Sumption, *Equality*, John Murray 1979, p. 43.
19. Alan Suggate, op. cit., p. 160.
20. Temple, op. cit., pp. 14–15.
21. Ibid., pp. 73–74.
22. Denys Munby, *God and the Rich Society*, Oxford University Press 1961, p. 157.
23. John Baillie, in presenting his Commission's Report to the General Assembly of the Church of Scotland 1942, in J. G. Riddell and George M. Dryburgh, *Crisis and Challenge*, Church of Scotland 1942, Appendix.
24. Baillie, *What is Christian Civilization?*, Oxford University Press 1945, p. 24.
25. Baillie, *God's Will for Church and Nation*, SCM Press 1946, p. 24.
26. Baillie, *God's Will*, p. 59.
27. Ibid., pp. 62, 156.
28. Ibid., p. 156.
29. J. G. Riddell and George M. Dryburgh, *Crisis and Challenge*, Church of Scotland 1942, p. 121.
30. Baillie, *God's Will*, p. 111.
31. Ibid., pp. 149–50.
32. Cf. E. R. Norman, *Church and Society in England, 1770–1970*, Oxford University Press 1976, pp. 372–77.
33. Lord Percy, *The Heresy of Democracy*, Eyre & Spottiswoode 1954, p. 337.

5. The Collapse of the Welfare Consensus

1. R. H. Tawney, *Equality*, p. 222.
2. Peter Townesend, *Poverty in the United Kingdom*, Penguin Books 1979, p. 895.
3. Frank Field, *Inequality in Britain: Freedom, Welfare and the State*, Collins, Fontana 1981, pp. 19ff.
4. David Donnison, *The Politics of Poverty*, pp. 7–8.
5. John Atherton, *The Scandal of Poverty: Priorities for the Emerging Church*, Mowbrays 1983, p. 38.
6. Peter Golding and Sue Middleton, *Images of Welfare*, Robertson 1982, pp. 160–200.
7. Ralph Harris and Arthur Seldon, *Over-ruled on Welfare*, IEA 1979.
8. Jeremy Seabrook, *What Went Wrong?*, Gollancz 1978.
9. Dexter Tiranti, 'The New Right: How it came about', *New Internationalist*, No. 133, 1984, p. 7.
10. Field, op. cit.
11. Richard Titmuss, *Commitment to Welfare*, Allen & Unwin 1968, p. 34, and Field, op. cit.
12. In Norman Mackenzie (ed.), *Conviction*, MacGibbon & Kee 1958, p. 63.
13. Julian Le Grand, *The Strategy of Equality: Redistribution and the Social Services*, Allen & Unwin 1982, p. 132.

14. J. C. Kincaid, *Poverty and Equality in Britain*, p. 217.
15. R. H. Tawney, *Equality*, p. 9.
16. Rudolph Klein, 'The Welfare State: A Self-inflicted Crisis', *The Political Quarterly*, vol. 51, 1980, pp. 24–34.
17. *The Economist*, 18 September 1982.
18. Lord Bauer, quoted in Digby Anderson, *The Kindness that Kills*, SPCK 1984, p. 99.
19. Arthur Seldon, *Wither the Welfare State*, IEA 1981, pp. 17–18.
20. Rhodes Boyson (ed.), *Down with the Poor*, Churchill Press 1971, p. 19.
21. Milton Friedman, *Free to Choose*, Penguin Books 1980, p. 125–6.
22. Brian Griffiths, *Morality and the Market Place*, Hodder & Stoughton 1982, p. 113.
23. Ibid., pp. 112–113.
24. Boyson, op. cit., p. 21.
25. Ibid., pp. 5–6.
26. See ibid., pp. 111f.
27. F. A. Hayek, *The Constitution of Liberty*, Routledge & Kegan Paul 1960, pp. 42–44.
28. Friedman, op. cit., p. 150.
29. On medicine see Alastair V. Campbell, *Medicine, Health and Justice*, Churchill Livingstone 1978, pp. 10–16.
30. Arthur Marwick, *Britain in the Century of Total War*, Penguin Books 1970, p. 430.

6. *The Public Role of the Church Today*

1. Anthony Sampson, *The Changing Anatomy of Britain*, Hodder & Stoughton 1982, p. xv.
2. John Habgood, *Church and Nation in a Secular Age*, Darton, Longman & Todd 1983, p. 45.
3. George Orwell, *The Lion and the Unicorn*, Penguin Books 1982, p. 91.
4. Francis Bridger, 'Mrs Thatcher's Beliefs', *Third Way*, July/August 1982, p. 9.
5. *The Times*, 27 January 1983.
6. Roger Scruton, *The Meaning of Conservatism*, Penguin Books 1980, p. 170.
7. Ibid., p. 171.
8. Ibid., pp. 171–2.
9. Ibid., p. 173.
10. Habgood, op. cit.
11. Ibid., p. 105.
12. Ibid.
13. Ibid., p. 61.
14. David Sheppard, *Bias to the Poor*, Hodder & Stoughton 1983.
15. Habgood, op. cit., p. 105.

7. From Welfare State to Welfare Society?

1. J. M. Keynes in Le Grand, *The Strategy of Equality*, Allen & Unwin, 1982, p. 139.
2. Joseph and Sumption, *Equality*, p. 11.
3. Ibid., p. 121.
4. Ibid., p. 123.
5. Ibid., pp. 27–8.
6. Peter Townsend and Nick Davidson, *Inequalities in Health: The Black Report*, Penguin Books 1982, p. 14.
7. Ibid., p. 39.
8. W. A. Robson, *Welfare State and Welfare Society*, Allen & Unwin 1976, p. 7.
9. Titmuss in Martin Loney, David Boswell and John Clarke, *Social Policy and Social Welfare*, Open University Press 1983, p. 18.
10. Norman Mackenzie (ed.), *Conviction*, MacGibbon & Kee 1958, p. 118.
11. Ibid., pp. 227, 229.
12. William Temple, *Christianity and Social Order*, p. 23.
13. Ibid., p. 54.
14. R. H. Preston, *Explorations in Theology 9*, SCM Press 1981, pp. 39–40.
15. W. A. Visser t'Hooft and J. H. Oldham, *The Church and Its Function in Society*, Allen & Unwin 1937, p. 210.
16. Forrester in Michael H. Taylor (ed.), *Christians and the Future of Social Democracy*, Hesketh Press 1982, p. 43.
17. Tawney, *The Acquisitive Society*, p. 223.
18. Le Grand, op. cit., p. 155.
19. Boyson in Loney, Boswell and Clarke, op. cit., p. 264.
20. Irving Kristol in Ramesh Mishra, *The Welfare State in Crisis*, Harvester Press 1984, p. 29.
21. Richard M. Titmuss, *Essays on 'The Welfare State'*, Allen & Unwin, 3rd edition 1976, pp. 82–3.
22. Enoch Powell in *Theology*, Vol. 85, 1982, p. 476.
23. F. von Hayek in Raymond Plant, Harry Lesser and Peter Taylor-Gooby, *Political Philosophy and Social Welfare*, Routledge & Kegan Paul 1980, p. 203.

Epilogue: Where Do We Go from Here?

1. Ramesh Mishra, *The Welfare State in Crisis*, pp. 109–20.
2. National Consumer Council, *Of Benefit to All: A Consumer Review of Social Security* 1984, p. 22.
3. R. Hadley and S. Hatch, *Social Welfare and the Failure of the State*, Allen & Unwin 1981, pp. 166–67.
4. NCC, op. cit., pp. 120–36.

Further Reading

A good recent reappraisal of the welfare state which gives detailed attention to possibilities of reform and improvement is Howard Glennerster (ed.), *The Future of the Welfare State: Remaking Social Policy* (Heinemann 1983). The essays are written from a Fabian standpoint and together form a useful introduction to the debate in social policy.

Frank Field's *Inequality in Britain: Freedom, Welfare and the State* (Collins, Fontana Paperbacks 1981) is an accessible and impressively argued explanation of 'what went wrong', together with proposals for reforms aimed at the eradication of poverty and the increase of freedom.

A brilliant and readable study of changing attitudes towards welfare and the poor in Britain and their effects upon legislation is Peter Golding and Sue Middleton's *Images of Welfare: Press and Public Attitudes to Poverty* (Martin Robertson 1982). This may be complemented by an impressionistic book full of important insights, *What Went Wrong? Working People and the Ideals of the Labour Movement* (Gollancz 1978), by Jeremy Seabrook.

The best and most forward-looking study of the role of the state in the provision of welfare is Roger Hadley and Stephen Hatch, *Social Welfare and the Failure of the State: Centralised Social Services and Participatory Alternatives* (Allen & Unwin 1981).

Ramesh Mishra's *The Welfare State in Crisis* (Wheatsheaf 1984) provides a useful, clear introduction to the theoretical issues and the positions of the New Right and the new, and not so new, Left, as well as making some suggestions about possible future developments. The theoretical discussion can be taken further in an important, but by no means elementary, book, *Political Philosophy and Social Welfare: Essays on the Normative Basis of Welfare Provision* by Raymond Plant, Harry Lesser and Peter Taylor-Goodby (Routledge and Kegan Paul 1980) or in Ramesh Mishra's *Society and Social Policy: Theories and Practice of Welfare* (Macmillan, 2nd edition 1981).

A standard history is Derek Fraser, *The Evolution of the British Welfare State* (Macmillan 1973).

Index

Index

Griffiths, Brian, 57

Habgood, John (Archbishop of York), 65, 72–5

Halsey, A. H., 62

Harris, Ralph (Lord), 57

Hayek, Friedrich von, 22, 30, 47, 57, 59, 85, 97

Institute of Economic Affairs, 56, 79

Jenkin, Patrick, 67, 83

Jenkins, David (Bishop of Durham), 75–6

Joseph, Sir Keith, 36, 60, 80f., 83

Keynes, John M., 22, 35f., 80

Keynesian economics, 20, 22, 44

King, Anthony, 94

Kingdom of God, viii, 3, 96ff.

Kristol, Irving, 94

Labour Party, 22f., 23ff., 33

Le Grand, Julian, 52–4, 92

Lindsay, A. D., 9

Luther, Martin, 69, 93

McDonald, J. I. H., ix

Machiavelli, 72

MacIntyre, Alasdair, 85

Market as provider of welfare, 95–6

Marxists, 87

Mayhew, Henry, 8

Means tests, 20, 54

Metz, J.-B., 69

Middle axioms, 36–8, 88–92

Middleton, Sue, 48f.

Munby, Denys, 38

Murdoch, Iris, 87

National Health Service, 19, 40, 61, 81ff.

New Left, attitudes to welfare, 55

New Right, 33, 47, 49f., 55–60, 64, 66, 67, 69, 86, 87, 94

Niebuhr, Reinhold, 7, 33, 34, 38

Norman, E. R., 43, 68f.

Nozick, R., 57, 85

Oldham, J. H., 34, 89

Orwell, George, 14, 28, 66, 94

Percy, Lord, Eustace, 42

Pluralism, 65

Poor Law, 8–10

Possessive individualism, 27, 32, 61, 80

Poverty, 8–11, 45–7, 52, 58f., 60, 77, 79, 82

Powell, Enoch, 96

Rawls, John, 84–5

Redistribution, 18, 20f., 23, 46, 49, 51, 53f., 58

Robson, William A., 86

Sampson, Anthony, 62

Scruton, Roger, 70–72, 73

Seabrook, Jeremy, 49

Second World War, 11ff., 34, 49

Seldon, Arthur, 56f.

Shalom, 3–5, 93f., 96, 98ff.

Sheppard, David, (Bishop of Liverpool), 75, 98–9

Smith, Adam, 35, 95–6

State, role of, 13f.;
as provider of welfare, 14, 17, 54, 57ff., 61, 78, 94;
'nanny state', 94

Sumption, Jonathan, 36, 80f., 83

Tawney, R. H., 10, 23f., 26–33, 34, 36, 43, 45, 52, 53, 80f., 85, 92

Taxation and welfare, 50–52

Temple, William (Archbishop of Canterbury), 1, 10, 17, 26, 32, 33ff., 43, 81, 87ff.

Thatcher, Margaret, 64, 66ff.

Thatcherism, 64, 67, 68

Thomson, David, 18

Tiranti, Dexter, 49–50

Titmuss, Richard, 16, 32, 45, 54, 85f., 95, 102

Townsend, Peter, 32, 45, 86

Toynbee Hall, 9

Unemployment, 10, 11, 25, 36, 47, 82